W9-CNC-451

Just ME

100 Monologues for Teens

Phyllis C. Johnson

MERIWETHER PUBLISHING LTD.
Colorado Springs, Colorado

Meriwether Publishing Ltd., Publisher
PO Box 7710
Colorado Springs, CO 80933-7710

www.meriwether.com

Editor: Theodore O. Zapel
Assistant editor: Nicole Rutledge
Cover design: Jan Melvin

© Copyright MMXIII Meriwether Publishing Ltd.
Printed in the United States of America
First Edition

All rights reserved. No part of this publication may be reproduced, stored in a retrieval system, or transmitted in any form or by any means, electronic, mechanical, photocopying, recording or otherwise, without permission of the publishers. The rights to unlimited amateur performances at one location of the monologues included in this book are granted with the purchase of this book. For performances at another location, a royalty fee of $10 per monologue performed must be remitted to Meriwether Publishing Ltd. (address above). The rights to perform these monologues apply to the purchaser and the purchasing organization only and may not be sold or transferred to any third party. All other rights including, without limitation, broadcast, radio, video, television and the rights of translation into foreign languages are controlled by the publisher, Meriwether Publishing Ltd. (address above).

NOTICE FOR PROFESSIONAL PRODUCTION
For any form of non-amateur presentation (professional, stage, radio, or television), permission must be obtained in writing from the publisher, Meriwether Publishing Ltd. (address above).

Library of Congress Cataloging-in-Publication Data

Johnson, Phyllis C.
 Just me : 100 monologues for teens / by Phyllis C. Johnson. --
First edition.
     pages cm
 ISBN 978-1-56608-190-0 (pbk.)
 1. Monologues--Juvenile literature. 2. Acting--Juvenile literature. [1.
Monologues. 2. Acting.] I. Title.
 PN2080.J64 2013
 812'.6--dc23
                                                         2012046587

1   2   3   13   14   15

30021006054845

Table of Contents

50

MONOLOGUES
FOR GUYS

1. The Coffee Maker

1   Be nice to me. I can be the first thing you see in the
2 morning. I jump-start the best of 'em. Two scoops of that
3 dark fragrant stuff, and I'm off and spurting out delicious
4 black brew. Some folks can't get along without me. It's nice
5 to feel needed — and I really feel needed. There's just one
6 thing that makes me nervous. It's the Keirug next door. I
7 mean, how can I compete with compact and tidy? Sure,
8 you'll find a filter with sometimes nasty moldy coffee dregs
9 in me days later, but I've got soul, baby. You can whip up
10 multiple cups of love with me. You can't do that with Guru
11 Keirug over there. It's a one-cup deal, I tell you. A one-way
12 street. It's every man for himself when it's coffee time. Isn't
13 a cup of joe more fun when it's shared with others? Spread
14 it around. Give the gift of warmth. Use me. Be more social
15 in the morning. You'll be glad you did. It's great sharing
16 stories over a hot cup. You might even be able to swap a cup
17 of coffee for the latest bestseller that your friend won't part
18 with. Heck, if you offer someone a chai latte, it might even
19 be worth all three books in the *Hunger Games* trilogy. Oh,
20 did I just strike a nerve? Books for a cup of java? How
21 about a stay in a timeshare for a nice cup? Or even a new
22 car? People who haven't had their caffeine in the morning
23 and really need it are apt to trade up for anything. I can be
24 like the goose with a golden egg. Think about it. You want
25 me on your counter. I'm the morning party waiting to
26 happen. The thing that percolates an idea whose time has
27 come for you. But that special moment when the brainstorm
28 comes needs to be shared over a cup of coffee. Coffee,
29 anyone?

2. About Race

1 (Has a piece of chalk in his pocket.)
2 Got a minute? Here's something that really bugs me. I
3 mean *really* bugs me. You know how when you take a test,
4 the standardized form asks you to check a little box to show
5 what race you are? I mean, what's up with that? My dad is
6 Asian and my mom is white. So do I check Asian or white?
7 It really isn't fair to have to choose like that. If I check white,
8 it's not fair to my dad. Checking Asian makes it unfair to
9 my mom, and she's the one who brought me into this world.
10 Kind of makes me feel like I'm betraying one or the other.
11 How can I do that? It sets up a feeling of angst, and the test
12 hasn't even started yet. So, Mr. Test Maker, think about it
13 before you put those little boxes on a test. It's just not fair.
14 You don't even have to do that when you take your dog to
15 the vet. There's no little box asking whether it's a black lab
16 or a poodle, and there's nowhere you can mark Labradoodle.
17 Are you following me here? Am I making sense? (Produces
18 chalk.) You see this piece of chalk in my hand? How about
19 if I just call myself Chalkasian? Nice ring to it, isn't it? If I'm
20 Chalkasian, maybe I can erase the first half of my life. That
21 wasn't so good anyway. Next time I'm taking a test, I'm
22 writing in Chalkasian. How does that sound? Does it work
23 for you?

3. Guilt

1   I can't believe I'm sitting here. What am I saying? I can't
2 believe Jeremy's in that box. Is everybody looking at me?
3 Maybe they think it's my fault. If only I'd gone to get that
4 ball instead of him. If only it had been me. Why didn't he
5 look before he crossed the street? They always tell us that.
6 He never listens. His room's a mess. It always is. I bet his
7 mama feels bad about always yelling at him. Look at her.
8 She's crying. Look at you, Jeremy. You can't even open your
9 eyes. We're dressed in suits, Jeremy. We never wear suits.
10 Except that one time when your aunt Carolyn took us to
11 church at Easter. Do you remember that time? We felt like
12 fish out of water, even though every guy around us was
13 wearing a suit. It just didn't feel natural. Thank goodness
14 that church lets people "come as they are" now. I'd much
15 rather wear jeans. How about you? Now there you are in a
16 suit, and so am I. They say image is everything but we're
17 still the same people inside, no matter how we're dressed.
18 Man, I still can't believe this. This can't be happening. I'll
19 pinch myself. That's it. This is nothing but a bad dream. Do
20 you think that's what it is? We're both having a bad dream?
21 This isn't real. It can't be real, can it? In a few minutes, I'm
22 going to wake up and find out that's what it is, and you and
23 me can go play ball again, Jeremy. Jeremy ... Jeremy?

4. The Arsonist

1   I didn't mean to do it. I really didn't. Standing back in
2   the crowd, I watched as the firefighters doused the flames.
3   One of many bystanders, I hoped no one noticed the guilt
4   on my face. The guilt that said, "Don't look at me, I didn't
5   mean to do it." Maybe it was the way my folks fought last
6   night. It could have been the fact that no one pays attention
7   to me. It's always Sheila, the one with perfect grades. The
8   perfect skin, the perfect everything. I don't know ... I look
9   down at my hands. They betrayed me. I'm not that kind of
10   kid. The one who lets his emotions get the best of him. I'm
11   no angel, I can assure you of that, but I am far from being
12   the devil. You might know me. I'm the kid next door. The
13   one who sat beside you on the bus that you never spoke to.
14   I might be the one you ignored at the lunch table or made
15   fun of when I did an oral report. It could have been your
16   house or your grandma's. It could have been your church or
17   your school. But it wasn't. It was my house. The place
18   where my parents raised me. The place where they gave my
19   sister birthday parties and forgot about mine. Told me that
20   boys are tough and they don't need fusses made over them.
21   The place where the dog got fed when I was often ignored.
22   See these tears? These tears staining my cheeks wash guilt
23   across my face because if I didn't feel so alone in my own
24   world, I wouldn't have done it. Can they fix someone like
25   me? Someone who played with a lighter Mom uses to light
26   her candles and accidentally lit a curtain? Well, maybe not
27   accidentally. Is anything really an accident? Is life a series
28   of events that were all planned by some unknown force as

1　we live our own free will? Predestination and free will. Do
2　they even belong in the same sentence?

5. The Artist

1   *(Holds an artist's paint brush.)*

2   I've been sitting here with my easel for days. Waiting to

3   catch the sun at just the right spot. Shining on the water.

4   Glimmering. *(Points.)* Look at that eagle over there. He

5   doesn't have any idea he's about to be captured. By me.

6   And I'm not even a hunter. See ... this brush is my spear.

7   I'll capture him in paint for everyone to see, and he's none

8   the wiser. Every shadow, every glimmer and every shine,

9   speaks to me. It calls my name. The breeze blows through

10 my hair and wakens my muse in a way that says, put paint

11 to canvas. I feel it run through my body and touch my soul,

12 begging for release through brush strokes. Blue tinged by

13 lavender swirls, wispy flocks of white through which a

14 brilliant sun peeks. Water in shades of gray and green wash

15 up marsh grass. Cattails wave to ducks swimming by, all

16 subjects in my creative court. Alone, yet not really, for the

17 host of nature beckons my call as I mix and swirl color,

18 destined for the canvas. I feel myself drift away in an

19 adrenaline rush. Forms take shape, and my vision slowly

20 comes to life in ecstasy only an artist could understand. I

21 roll the brush between my fingers, gazing upwards at the

22 sky. A misty rain touches my cheek, and I glance down at

23 my palette. Not wanting to dilute the paint, it's wrap it up

24 or watch oil and water mix like the state of my emotions. To

25 be so charged up for creative release and have to pack it up

26 ... oh, man. The wind shifts, the rain stops, and the

27 pounding of my heart subsides. You see ... the painting is

28 everything, and I am lost in it. Nothing else matters. I refuse

1 to be pulled away by a whim of Mother Nature. I throw
2 myself back into my brush strokes. A touch-up here, a
3 shading there, a highlighting just so ... ahhhh, the kind of
4 gratification only an artist knows. If you aspire to my task,
5 then you'll need a fire burning in you like last fall's weenie
6 roast. Fan the flame. You can never let it go out. Follow your
7 dreams and never give up. Never.

6. The Clock Maker

1   Well, it's about time you came in. Welcome to my world.
2 Time's my game, and it just keeps spinning around. Today
3 is the tomorrow you worried about yesterday, and all that.
4 While you might not wear a watch like your old folks, that
5 clock on your iPhone keeps you informed of the time. What
6 everybody still seems to need is a clock on the wall. That's
7 where I come in. Do you really think that all clocks are made
8 in factories? Nope. I hand make these puppies. Bring me
9 your grandmother's china plate and I'll make a clock out of
10 it, one that will mean something to you years down the road.
11 And recyclables, I can make a clock out of them, too. Old
12 tired records, a drink bottle, just about anything can be
13 made into a clock. Don't look at me like I'm crazy. It's true.
14 I guarantee you'll look at everything around you differently
15 now that you realize that the clock is ticking on our planet
16 and we need to reuse and reinvent. Tick, tick, tick, tick,
17 tick. Uh-oh, what time is it? Time for me to get back to work
18 ... It's all about time, you know ...

7. The Gym Instructor

1   My name's Rex. I can either be your best friend or your
2 worst nightmare. See those machines over there? You're
3 going to do sets of workouts until you cry for mercy. No, I'm
4 not mean; this is in your best interest. OK, grab that bar
5 and pull yourself up, holding your knees even with your
6 chest. You can do it. That's right. See, you're doing it. OK,
7 now hold it there and count to ten. Hey, don't look at me
8 like that. Like I said, this is in your best interest. I've always
9 wanted to help people reach their physical maximum
10 performance. Why, even when I was little, I did things to
11 make my mom chase me. Sure, I was a little hellion, but she
12 was getting a workout. I was always thinking of her, of
13 course. Then, when I took my brother's marbles and he
14 chased me down, again, I was just giving him a good
15 workout. Hey, any means possible. That's what I do to push
16 you. If I have to go out and buy a Starbucks gift card to
17 push you into exercising, I'll do that. But no, wait a minute,
18 how many calories are in a cup of their joe? Anyway, back
19 to exercising. It's good for your heart, your mind, and your
20 mood. Get on that treadmill and see if your heart rate
21 doesn't pick up. Exercise awhile and see what cool thoughts
22 can come your way. Who knows, you might even invent
23 something in that cranium of yours while you're on the
24 elliptical machine. As for your mood, I personally don't see
25 many people leaving the gym with a frown on their face. It
26 helps get rid of stress. Give it a shot. You won't be
27 disappointed. OK, now that we have all that straight,
28 there's something else I want to talk to you about. But first
29 ... sit up straight.

8. The Jeweler

1   I see some of you have rings that are too tight. I can fix
2 that, you know. Resizing them isn't a problem for me. Just
3 come on by. Now, if some of you remove your rings for some
4 other reason, well, I can't help you there. Maybe the
5 counselor down the street ... uh, never mind. OK, so back
6 to what I was saying ... I'm a jeweler. If you've got broken
7 jewelry, I can fix it like new. I'll take those pieces and shine
8 them like nobody's business. If you have stones that fell
9 out, I can fix them faster than you can say Kim Kardashian.
10 You know the expression "diamonds are a girl's best
11 friend?" It's true. Just ask a girl with a rock on her hand.
12 The sparkles match the ones in her eye. Is it worth it, fellas?
13 You bet your bottom dollar it's worth it. Ever seen some guy
14 getting dragged into the jewelry store by a girl with that
15 gleam in her eye? I see it happen all the time. You can't deny
16 that sometimes dragging is the right term to use. But think
17 of how happy it'll make her. I mean truly. Not to mention
18 how happy it'll make me. Uh-oh. Did I just say that out
19 loud? But hey, I got bills to pay.

9. The Pianist

1   *(A toy piano or keyboard is On-stage.)*
2   Music is life and life is music. Wait a minute, that's so
3 cliché. What can I say to you to let you know how much
4 music means to me? Maybe I could sing. Would that
5 convince you? Maybe I can play a guitar and have you up out
6 of your chair dancing. Would that convince you? What will it
7 take for you to see how huge music is in my world? This
8 piano is to me what a race car is to its driver. It's the grape
9 jelly to my peanut butter. It's the chocolate to my s'more.
10 It's the ying to my yang. My love affair with music started
11 when I was very young. It must have been the toy baby
12 grand piano my mom bought me. All I remember is this ...
13 one touch of middle C, and I was sold. One touch, that's all
14 it took. The funny thing was that middle C sent out enough
15 vibration to cut off the furnace thermostat that hung right
16 above the piano. I'd sit in there and practice to my heart's
17 content until my mom came in the room asking me to stop.
18 "Stop practicing," she'd say. "It's getting cold in here."
19 Unless you're in love with music, you won't get it. If I'm
20 having a crappy day, all I need to do is sit down and play
21 my blues away. It makes me happy. I ask you, has
22 Schroeder in Peanuts ever looked unhappy when playing the
23 piano? Wait a minute, maybe that's not a good comparison.
24 He doesn't pick up his head, does he? Oh, whatever ... now,
25 where was I? Oh yeah, it floats my boat. Soothes my
26 frazzled nerves. What more can I say? *(Turns back to audience*
27 *and plays on a toy piano.)*

10. The Photographer

1   Last night I shot a family down by the river. No, I'm not
2   a murderer, and no, I'm not going to jail. I shot them with
3   my trusty Pentax. No pent-up anger here. No wrath or
4   venom behind this lens. Just as you might expect,
5   everybody was dressed alike. Baby blue T-shirts and khakis.
6   It was a real trick getting everybody to smile at one time. A
7   real trick. When Mom looked relaxed enough, Dad looked
8   like he had an ax to grind with somebody. Then I got the
9   parents to laugh and smile again, and Junior seemed to
10   have his mind on his date last night. He was a million miles
11   away. The baby, otherwise known as a late surprise, was
12   intent on digging her shoe through the dirt, causing a nasty
13   mess. The middle child looked alternately between parents,
14   but not at me. With all that said, just call me the Miracle
15   Worker. Next time you see a big family portrait hanging over
16   somebody's mantel, think of me. You have no idea what it
17   took to get them to look like that. A sitting fee, my foot. The
18   baby was doing anything but sitting. Maybe I should call it
19   a chasing fee. That's more like it. Yeah ... now excuse me
20   while I go back to work. Smile ... let me see those pearly
21   whites.

11. The Candy Peddler

1   People love me. They really do. Is it me or the candy I
2 sell? That's a good question. They love me. Especially the
3 women. Who can resist a guy with chocolate? I'm not even
4 the best-looking guy in town, but when I'm standing there
5 offering free samples of fudge, I'm suddenly as popular as
6 George Clooney. It works, guys, trust me. Why, just the
7 other day I saw this good-looking girl going by. She seemed
8 to have something heavy on her mind. I couldn't catch her
9 eye, but as soon as I said, "Like a piece of fudge?" she
10 turned that pretty head in my direction and smiled. Just like
11 putty in my hand. Dark chocolate really gets 'em. Besides,
12 they say that it's good for you. Healthy and able to send
13 women into ecstasy. It doesn't get any better than that. If I
14 pull out the Divinity Fudge, the reaction is divine. Pull out
15 peanut butter fudge, and they go nuts. Offer them Rocky
16 Road, and the path to their hearts is made smooth. I've got
17 all kinds of treats for your sweet tooth. Maybe the gummy
18 worms don't sound so romantic or alluring, but they win
19 hearts. Some go for the nostalgic candies. Pop Rocks even
20 rocked somebody's world. Remember those chunks of
21 explosive fun that bounce around in your mouth? I'm telling
22 you, there's nothing like 'em. And then there are certain Life
23 Savers that glow in the dark when you bite down on them.
24 Amazing, huh? One of my favorites is the caramel with the
25 sugar center. I like punching out the sugar to eat first, and
26 then I eat the caramel. It's almost as much fun as the little
27 wax bottles of juice or the candy necklaces. Of course, I
28 wouldn't wear one ... I'm just sayin'. I could go on and on

1   about the joy of candy. The enthusiasm you see here is real
2   and genuine, just like the rush you get when you take a bite
3   into a truffle. Ooooh, did I just see you take a step
4   backwards? I knew I'd get you!

12. The Taxi Driver

1   Talk fast because the meter is running. OK, where is it
2   you want to go? Timbuktu? Or do you want to see the
3   aurora borealis? Maybe the Eiffel Tower? Your wish is my
4   command. Just make sure you pay the piper when you
5   climb onto my magic carpet ride. I know my way around.
6   You're basically paying for my gas and my knowledge of the
7   road system. If you're in New York, you're really paying for
8   my tuition in the School of Hard Knocks when it comes to
9   driving. Defensive driving is what I call it. Every man for
10 himself. It's a dog-eat-dog world out there for some of us. If
11 you find me in the Dominican Republic, I might be one of
12 the taxi drivers lining up near the cruise ships, offering to
13 take you to see a waterfall. Or you might find me outside an
14 airport in the United Kingdom, offering to take you to see
15 Buckingham Palace. Part of the perks is looking in the
16 rearview mirror, watching your expression when you see
17 things you've never seen before. Maybe it's kind of a
18 vicarious thrill, living through someone else's eyes. I can be
19 part of something special. I've seen wedding proposals, I've
20 seen women deliver babies. Heaven help me. There aren't
21 many things I haven't seen while driving people around. Call
22 me a multi-tasker, if you will. Finagling the traffic jams,
23 listening to the dispatcher, and being mindful of the
24 passengers in the backseat at the same time. I can rescue
25 you from walking in circles in Washington D.C. and get you
26 back to your hotel in a flash. My job as a taxi driver can be
27 taxing at times, but I am not sitting in one spot all day long,
28 and that makes it all worth it. OK, would you look at that?

1   Here we are. You've reached your destination. And all in one
2   piece. Don't forget your bag, and by the way ... don't forget
3   I accept tips.

13. The Ticket Taker

1   You might not know me, but I'm the ticket taker. You
2 know, the one who tears off the stub at the movie theater.
3 The one who can make or break your entry back into the
4 theater if you have to go potty. I find out real quick who
5 knows left from right. I should be the one to quiz you when
6 you're applying for a job. One wrong move, and bam, sorry
7 Charlie, no job for you. I get a kick out of telling people,
8 "Third door down on the right" and then watching them go
9 to the second door on the left. Happens every time. And if
10 you only knew how many huge tubs of popcorn have passed
11 by me. I could get high cholesterol just sniffing the fumes.
12 Honestly, I wonder if breathing it does anything to clog the
13 arteries. The fun part is watching folks come out of a movie
14 either laughing or crying. Sometimes they look scared.
15 Sometimes they show no emotion at all, and I try to
16 remember which movie they came out of so I'll make sure
17 not to go to that one. I guess the least fun part of my job
18 is cleaning up after everybody. Have you ever picked up wet
19 popcorn? I mean, what is up with that? I've considered
20 bringing my dog with me to work. He'd take care of the
21 edible mess in a heartbeat. Maybe that's not such a bad
22 idea. Excuse me, I think I've got to go home and get my
23 dog.

14. I Want a Job

1   Heard of any good jobs lately? Anything? I'll even wash
2   windows. Did you hear me? *I'll even wash windows!* Let's
3   see, how many places have I applied to? Hmmmm, it must
4   have been thirty. Just call me a chameleon. I have resumes
5   that list so many different things, you'd think that surely I
6   must be schizo. Yeah, I've applied to meter maid, popcorn
7   maker at the movies, pottery person down at Paint 'Em Up
8   and childcare person down at Child's Play. How can I
9   possibly be qualified for so many widely varied jobs? Well,
10   you see, what I do is imagine myself spending the money
11   made at the job, and that catapults me into an acting role
12   that you wouldn't believe. That's what it's all about. Acting
13   the part. Or rather, fake it 'til you make it. Keep that in
14   mind. Want a certain job? Let 'em think you know all there
15   is to know about it. As you go through life, you're going to
16   meet a lot of people cast in roles for which they've had no
17   training. They just won't let you know it. They've become
18   good at acting the part of someone who appears to know
19   what they're doing and getting paid some good money in the
20   process. So go for it. Send out those applications and wait
21   to be surprised. Reach for the stars. You just might touch
22   one. Now if you'll excuse me, I have to go fill out an
23   application.

15. New Calendar

1   There's something special about getting a new calendar,
2   isn't there? It means a new year, a new chance at life,
3   turning over a new leaf. There are resolutions to be made
4   and goals to be met. Whether it's eating right or exercise,
5   we're all determined that this year will be the year we
6   become our best possible selves. The self that gets in
7   shape, gets healthy, and gets that perfect job. I hold in my
8   hands a new calendar. Big blocks for filling in. Parties to go
9   to, dates to remember, the SAT. Do we want our lives
10 dictated by clocks and time? Just how can we enjoy
11 ourselves when we're always checking to see if we're where
12 we're supposed to be at a certain time? Man, I seem to be
13 contradicting myself. How can I be excited about the
14 possibilities of filling in a new calendar yet feel bound by too
15 many penciled-in dates? You can't have it two ways. Like
16 having your cake and eating it, too. While I want fun
17 weekends, I need time to chill. How do you do it? How do
18 you go all you want and yet stay relaxed and chilled? Is
19 there any way to pull that off? Is that too tall an order? Am
20 I the Energizer Bunny? Can I keep on going like this? What's
21 going to recharge *my* battery? Is my goal this year learning
22 how to say no? Not to join too many clubs or go to too many
23 events? Is the answer really to sit at home and stare at a
24 blank calendar, yet feel rested? Rested and bored or busy
25 and tired. Take your pick. It seems you get one or the other.
26 Happy New Year.

16. The Philanthropist

1   *(Enters with a bag of groceries, which he sets on the floor.)*
2   I like helping people. It makes me feel good. Being a
3   philanthropist has its advantages. It gives you a warm fuzzy,
4   but it also helps others. There are tons of stingy people in the
5   world, but at the end of the day, whose lives have they made
6   better? Imagine yourself standing on a sidewalk looking up at
7   the many skyscraper apartments in a big city. There are so
8   many stories out there. Look at the windows that you see
9   open, no curtains. If their lives were as open a book as the
10 windows into which you peek, you'd know that there are a lot
11 of hurting and hungry souls. Someone needs to help them.
12 Somebody needs to care about whether or not they have food
13 on their table or shoes to wear. Who is that someone going at
14 be? There are many groups you can help with. I choose to help
15 with a group that feeds people. I donate money to this cause.
16 Like, how many steaks and baked potatoes can I eat anyway?
17 There are more zeroes in my bank account than donut holes
18 down at Dunkin' Donuts. What am I going to do with all that
19 money? It's only fair that I share some of it. And so I visit the
20 farmers and buy their excess crops and carry it down to the
21 local community center once a month. People show up and
22 volunteer to help bag it up and distribute it to those who don't
23 have much. You should see the looks of gratitude on their
24 faces. Well, maybe not so much for the rutabagas or turnips in
25 their bags, but for everything else. If I was in their shoes, I'd
26 want someone to do the same for me. Like the old expression,
27 "If it feels good, do it." I rest my case. The rest is history. Help
28 somebody. You'll be glad you did. *(Picks up a bag of groceries*
29 *and walks away.)*

17. The Poet

1   I need one more word to finish this poem. It has to be a
2 good word. Not just one that rhymes for the sake of
3 rhyming; that way it feels forced. Being a poet brings its
4 share of challenges. OK, so this might be a fluff job to some
5 people, but for me, it's serious business. I go to poetry
6 slams and compete with the best of 'em. The folks who
7 drive in from other states for the competition are out for
8 blood. I'm telling you, they mean business. They memorize
9 every line and know how to present their stuff. I'm in awe of
10 the ones who come across like a preacher at a podium.
11 Maybe some of them have missed their calling. Preacher
12 poets, that's what I call them. I haven't always gone to
13 poetry slams. I first started out reading poems to folks at
14 work during lunch. One guy took off at lunch saying he
15 couldn't take it anymore. That's when I knew that I needed
16 to perfect my technique. Anybody can stand and read a
17 poem. That's not what it's all about. You have to *feel* it. You
18 have to become that poem. You have to eat, sleep, and
19 breathe that poem. Am I making sense here? Are you
20 reading me loud and clear? Don't just stand up there and
21 read off the page. Make eye contact with those watching
22 you. Let your words reach down into their souls, pulling up
23 their guts, make them squirm. If you've touched a nerve,
24 then you've done your job. Memorize the lines. Make it
25 matter. The next time you project yourself with one of your
26 poems, wow them with your charisma. Let them walk away
27 feeling that they have truly experienced you and your poetry.
28 Make it rock. It'll make you rock. Trust me.

18. The Produce Stocker

1   You there ... eat healthy. Let me say that again, eat
2 healthy. What's that I see in your purse? M&M's? Little
3 Debbie cake? Some Ho Hos? Dump it out. Every last piece
4 of it. Get in your car and drive down to the grocery store.
5 You know, the place that has the food that's best for you on
6 the aisles that border the walls? Let's stop for a minute and
7 think about what's sitting in those aisles. Green stuff.
8 Orange stuff. Red stuff. The kind of stuff that you cut up on
9 a cutting board. There's also the white and yellow stuff.
10 Usually on the far opposite wall. Some cow had her teats
11 squeezed like crazy for those grocery items. Really good
12 things don't come easy. Just ask a cow. Anything on the
13 aisles in between is bleached, mixed, and processed to
14 death. Am I right? Have you ever looked at the ingredients
15 on the boxes? All those words that you can't pronounce are
16 an indication that maybe it's not so good for your body. Try
17 eating from just those walls bordering the aisles for a week.
18 If it's not fresh, don't eat it. If it's not white or orange, don't
19 drink it. And to that white, thick, and creamy stuff that's
20 sometimes topped with granola, I say, *yo!* Think about
21 what's in those mixes and boxes. Preservatives. MSG. Don't
22 you want to preserve yourself? Wanna be around to see your
23 grandchildren? How about the great-grandchildren? Do you
24 want to have arteries clogged up like the downtown tunnel
25 at rush hour? Huh? What's that you say? I can't hear you ...

19. The Realtor

1   I wonder why they call it real estate. As opposed to
2   unreal estate? Maybe now it should be known as surreal
3   estate. Doesn't surreal mean something that you can hardly
4   believe? Well, the prices of houses have surely been surreal.
5   I have the glorious job of showing you from house to house.
6   Isn't that the way it's done? Here's the trick. You see, what
7   we do is take you to the worst dump imaginable. Once
8   you're thoroughly grossed out, we take you to the most
9   expensive house out there. It'll wow you, but you will have
10   no doubt in your mind that you can't afford it. The next
11   thing we do is take you to a house more suited to you in
12   price and size. This ploy will have you feeling like Goldilocks.
13   The first house was too small, the next was too big, and this
14   one will look just right. It tells your brain, *This is it. This is
15   it!* That way, it saves me a lot of driving because you will
16   immediately think that surely this is the house of your
17   dreams, just waiting for you. Next time you go looking for
18   houses, see if this isn't true. Don't say I didn't warn you.
19   Oh, and in case I'm the one showing you the houses, forget
20   I ever said this. I have only the best motives in mind. Always
21   and forever. Now if you'll excuse me, I've got to do some
22   house scouting.

20. The Repo Guy

1   I'm the guy you love to hate. I get shot at. Bad things
2   are said to me. There are death threats on my phone at
3   home. I need eyes in the back of my head when I go out at
4   night. I'm the repo guy. You know, the one who comes to
5   your house when you're not looking and repossesses your
6   car because you're behind in payments. It's not a pretty
7   job, but somebody has to do it. It feels like stealing, and
8   maybe if the truth be known, I have a little bit of
9   kleptomaniac in me that gets fed this way. Who knows? The
10   last car I had to repo was a yellow convertible. Some old
11   lady with dementia had forgotten to make her payments. We
12   kept sending notices to her house, but she kept ignoring
13   them. If we had known she had dementia, maybe somebody
14   could have helped her. She was looking out her lacy white
15   kitchen curtains when I did the dirty deed. As I pulled out
16   of the driveway, I saw her come hobbling out the front door
17   with her walker, yelling some not-so-pretty things in my
18   direction. I did feel kind of bad about doing that. I didn't
19   know the owner was going to look like my grandma. That
20   stung. It's an ugly job, but one that has to be done. Another
21   repo job that sticks out was when I repossessed a tractor.
22   That man named John didn't think I was such a dear when
23   I drove off with his prized green possession. You should have
24   seen his face. The furrows were as deep as the last rows he
25   planted. It was a shame, really. It wasn't his fault. It was the
26   lack of rain. And then I went and rained on his parade. The
27   real culprit here was Mother Nature. Maybe we should have
28   sent her a bill. Repo man. An ugly job. But somebody has
29   to do it.

21. The Runner

1   I'm addicted. I admit it. Running is in my blood now.
2   Even if it's ugly outside, I have to be out there. I need that
3   rush coursing through my blood. I need whatever it is that
4   comes over me when I reach the state where I don't even
5   feel my body anymore. Have you ever felt it? Isn't it like
6   something you've never felt otherwise? OK, maybe it
7   compares to eating a York Peppermint Patty. Well, not quite.
8   The pavement has become my friend, but my brain hasn't
9   told my knees that one day it might not be the case. When
10   I'm running, I'm one with the road. I lose myself in the
11   moment. It has become my lover. I go out to meet it every
12   day with anticipation that I will get my fix. Nothing else can
13   compete. With shorts and tank top, I greet the day, eager to
14   join my muse in our morning run. With water bottle in hand,
15   it begins. I see others having the same love affair, and we
16   give each other a raised eyebrow as we pass each other. It
17   takes too much effort when running to raise a hand, but
18   they understand. Same sign of concentration on their faces,
19   we sprint on parallel universes. It's the great uniting factor.
20   No matter what kind of job they have, what kind of house
21   they live in, what kind of car they drive, we are on an even
22   playing field. Two people and the pavement, where feet meet
23   ground in a frenzied attempt to get the same natural high
24   we've gotten the day before. But oh, it feels so good. *(Turns*
25   *and runs off the stage.)*

22. The Screenwriter

1   For every movie you've ever been to, there's a
2 screenwriter behind the scenes. Well, maybe not really
3 behind the scenes, but somewhere on the premises, if they
4 want to see the outcome of their hard work. Did you know
5 that screenwriters can earn as much as a thousand dollars
6 a page? That's nothing to sneeze at. Sure is more money
7 than what I made when I sold a poem for five bucks. There's
8 a lot to be considered though. It once took me about five
9 years to come up with enough money to make a movie.
10 There's more to this job than sitting behind a keyboard.
11 Yep, a whole lot more. I have to carve out blocks of time to
12 write. That means no watching *American Idol*. No watching
13 *Survivor*. No watching *House Hunters*. Nope. If I want to pay
14 for my house and be someone's idol, I've got to sit, butt in
15 chair, and write like nobody's business. If you have a dream,
16 you have to follow it. And if you have great dreams, you have
17 to write them down. You never know when last night's
18 dream might win you an Emmy award. You have to keep a
19 notebook by your bed. How do you think *Silence of the*
20 *Lambs* got birthed? Ugh, sorry about that. Yeah, I realize
21 some of you just ate and maybe that wasn't the best movie
22 to talk about right after dinner. But hey, that's what we
23 screenwriters think about. What will make them hurl their
24 cookies? What will make them sit on the edge of their seats
25 or lose sleep over? We ask ourselves the big question, "What
26 if?" That is what spins the wheels and greases our gears.
27 Just ask any screenwriter. They'll tell you that it's the thing
28 the best story is made of. Get it? I think you do. Oops, it's
29 time for butt in chair. Now if you'll excuse me ...

23. The Sheriff

1   Sometimes they call me a County Monty. It's kind of got
2   a nice ring to it, but I haven't decided if I like it or not. Sort
3   of makes me sound like a hick. The jury's still out about
4   whether I should be complimented or insulted. If you see me
5   on the interstate and you're broken down, I'm your best
6   friend. If I pull you over when you're speeding, I'm your
7   worst nightmare. You never know just how we'll meet. I'd
8   love to be everybody's hero, but I can't always say that's so.
9   See this badge I wear? It's a five-point star. I've even had
10 people ask me if it's the Star of David. Well, my name is
11 David and it's my star badge, so I guess you could say, yes,
12 it's the Star of David. I've always wanted a badge. When I
13 was a little boy, I had a badge on my shirt when we played
14 cops and robbers. I'd get on my bike, and we'd put
15 clothespins and cardboard on the tires so they'd make a
16 cool flapping noise when I rode. I'd make the siren sound
17 with my mouth so the other kids would know that they'd
18 have to pull over, and I'd give them a ticket for speeding. Of
19 course, I'm telling you all this in confidence. You're not to
20 tell any of your neighbors what I'm saying. If I pull them over
21 to write them a ticket, they'd bring up the story about my
22 bike and the cardboard flappers, and I'd be bound to shed
23 the stiff upper lip I wear when I pull someone over. I mean,
24 how could you write someone a ticket when they have you
25 laughing? It's just not going to happen. So, when you see
26 this badge now, just think about the seriousness of my job.
27 If you make me laugh, I may have to arrest you. I'm not
28 joking. Hey, wipe that smile off your face. Where's my pad
29 of tickets?

24. The Shoe Repairman

1   You there. Have any shoes you need repairing? Repair.
2 That's right. Repair. Have you ever heard of such a thing?
3 Believe it or not, some people actually get their shoes
4 repaired. This isn't a hundred percent society of
5 throwaways. Some things are meant to be fixed and saved.
6 What if your future husband decided to throw you away? Uh,
7 uh-oh, I forgot about divorce. Um, never mind. That's not a
8 good comparison. How about if somebody decided to throw
9 away their good name? Uh, I guess they do that, too.
10 Hmmmm, let's see. What do people throw away? Love,
11 second chances, a better job? If only I hadn't let her slip
12 away. And yes, she gave me a second chance. If only I'd
13 taken that better job offer. I could just kick myself. But I
14 can't because I'm not wearing good butt-kicking shoes, and
15 on top of that, these need repairing. That's something I'm
16 good at. Not so good at repairing a relationship. They don't
17 send you to school to learn that. Maybe they should. It
18 might make a difference in the divorce rate. Sorry, I'm just
19 venting. I can't help it. Life sucks sometimes. I'm just
20 sayin'. But if I stay busy enough, maybe I'll forget about her.
21 Yeah, that's it. I'll work hard. I can stay busy fixing shoes.
22 You there, got any shoes you want fixed? Do you? Huh?

25. The Superstitious Person

1   *(A calendar is on the wall. Stands holding an umbrella.)*
2   Mama always told me not to open an umbrella in the
3   house. I guess it's supposed to give you bad luck or
4   something. I try to be really careful when I'm holding a
5   mirror, too, so I won't drop it and ruin my life for the next
6   seven years. As for seeing a black cat cross my path, I'd run
7   over it first. There, problem solved. *(Pause)* Uh-oh, I see you
8   gasping out there. Do you really think I'd run over the poor
9   kitty? And like it would even hurt it. Don't you know that
10 cats have nine lives? Anyway, my mom also told me that
11 the first visitor who comes to my house on New Year's Day
12 is supposed to be someone of the male persuasion. And
13 exactly what am I supposed to do if a woman shows up? Tell
14 her to go away? I come from the most superstitious family
15 you'll ever meet. A lot of it I ignore, but you won't see me
16 walking under a ladder. I have a phobia for those things
17 anyway. I'm thinking maybe in another lifetime I must have
18 fallen off one. Maybe for good luck, I'll throw salt over my
19 shoulder. But wait a minute, is that good luck or bad luck?
20 I don't remember. Now, speaking of ladders, I have to hit
21 the sack. I have to have painters over tomorrow. *(Checks*
22 *calendar.)* It's Friday *(Checks calendar again.)* the 13th, oh no!
23 *(Freaks and runs out.)*

26. The Tattoo Artist

1   So you want a tattoo, huh? Well, you've come to the
2   right place. Have a seat in this chair right here. Look at the
3   wall over there. We have all kinds of tattoos. Butterflies,
4   flowers, hearts. If you're feeling rough and tough, we have
5   skulls and dagger tattoos. The choices are almost endless.
6   I see you wrinkling your forehead. Who likes pain, anyway?
7   I know I sure don't. That was the downside to it. It'll burn
8   for a while. I won't lie about it. So what's the big deal about
9   getting one, anyway? What's the attraction? That's what
10   people ask me. For guys in the military, it's like a rite of
11   passage. How many military guys do you know who have
12   one? Maybe it's losing some of its stigma. Maybe not so
13   Hell's Angels to get one these days. Even the Hell's Angels
14   have a better name now. And some of the most goth kids
15   you'd meet are some of the nicest. So have you made up
16   your mind yet? What's your pleasure? Have you picked out
17   a tattoo? Think hard. It's going to be with you a long, long
18   time. When you're an eighty-year-old lady, how's that tattoo
19   going to look with a few time-kissed wrinkles running
20   through it? What's your grandson gonna say if he sees a
21   tattoo that says, "Cougar?" When you're a seventy-year-old
22   guy married to Marie, what's she going to think about your
23   tattoo in a private spot that says Stephanie? Think long and
24   hard about it. Just think of me as someone who's helping
25   write your life story, because this tattoo is going to be your
26   present, past, and future. Thought it over now? All set?
27   *(Light fades to the sound of something sizzling like a brand.)*

27. The Touch

1   I was sitting in the commons talking to some guys when
2 I first saw her. Long legs, long brown hair, eyes that sparkle
3 like she's up to something. Man. I tried to not let the guys
4 see who I was looking at. I sure don't need any competition.
5 Too late. I hadn't moved my gaze quick enough. Bill caught
6 my glance and looked in her direction. "Ummmm," was all
7 he had to say, with a big smile on his face. "She's off
8 limits," I told him. Then I tried to carry on the conversation
9 without missing a beat. It didn't work. All six sets of male
10 eyes drifted her way. She was trying to catch up with some
11 girls headed to the tardy table. In class later, I just couldn't
12 get her off my mind. What was it about her? At lunch, I saw
13 her again. Again, she was alone, but trying to catch up with
14 others. She'd gotten her lunch late. The lunch table she was
15 headed for had just finished eating and was getting up to
16 leave. Then she spotted me. I was looking at her. She was
17 looking at me. Then it happened. She walked over to my
18 table, leaned over, and touched me on the shoulder. There
19 was something in her touch. I can't describe it. It sent
20 electricity through my body. I saw myself coming and going.
21 It was as though we were in a time machine. I envisioned
22 myself dating this girl, and she'd only just touched me.
23 What was in that touch? Was there something magical? Had
24 it pierced through my very soul? Something in me united
25 with her in a single touch. It was like nothing I'd ever felt.
26 I've heard of love at first sight. What about love at first
27 touch?

28. The Umbrella

1   (*Enters with comic strip umbrella as described below.*)
2   At first we didn't notice it. The umbrella in the stand by
3 the front door. When we bought the house, it was there. I
4 guess someone had left it behind. It was a cool-looking
5 umbrella, really. It had a cool comic strip design on it. What
6 better way to brighten up a rainy day than with a comic
7 strip? The comic strip was the one where Snoopy is typing
8 a story. He's beginning it with, "It was a dark and stormy
9 night." One of the other characters comes in and fusses at
10 him about starting his story like that. As a writer, that
11 always strikes me as funny. At first, I didn't realize the
12 powers this umbrella possessed. The first day I used it when
13 it was raining, I really didn't give much thought to how it
14 might influence me. I had to go to a funeral. I was wearing
15 black like almost everyone else. The cemetery was dotted
16 with blue and black umbrellas. Then I showed up with this
17 comic strip umbrella. At first no one noticed. Then they
18 heard me laughing. I don't know what possessed me to
19 break out in a laugh. It was a funeral, for crying out loud. It
20 must have been the umbrella. It definitely had powers.
21 Before long, it spread. It was almost contagious. Sniffing
22 turned into snickering and long faces turned into laughter.
23 "It was a dark and stormy night," read one little boy,
24 reading my umbrella out loud. He was old enough to read
25 but young enough to not realize it was not the time and
26 place to display his reading ability. With that, the minister
27 just gave it up. He put down his Bible, slapped his legs, and
28 let out a belly laugh. "Our late friend is going where there

1   **will be no more dark and stormy nights," he said. It was a**
2   **real moment. All because of the umbrella.** *(Opens umbrella*
3   *and walks Off-stage.)*

29. The Butcher

1   Two words. Raw meat. It's my life's blood. Sounds gory,
2 doesn't it? No, I'm not a vampire. There's no such thing. I'm
3 a butcher. Knives are my friend. The sharper, the better.
4 And the meat slicer, I have an even tighter bond with that.
5 And it's gotta be sharp. There's no other way. Super sharp.
6 Sharp enough to split a hair. Sharp enough to pass the bar
7 exam on the first try. Well, you get the picture. If blood is a
8 sign of a crime committed, then this place is reeking with
9 trouble. I suppose someone could get murdered in here and
10 no one would be on to it. On any given day, there's lot of
11 blood oozing around here. I try to keep it cleaned up so no
12 one gets grossed out. The other day a woman came in and
13 asked for a London broil. She wanted a pretty one. Pretty.
14 Now, is that a word for a piece of meat? You bet your booty
15 it is. If you don't get a pretty piece of meat, then when you
16 cook it, it's gonna be full of fat and gristle. It's gotta be
17 pretty. I'm not kidding. This is where my know-how comes
18 in. Got a question about meat? I'm your guy. I can steer you
19 in the right direction. Oh, sorry for the pun. I couldn't help
20 myself. It comes with the territory. Have a question about
21 strip steak or chuck roast? Chucking all jokes aside, I'll tell
22 you which cuts are the best for your recipe. It's a recipe for
23 success, I tell you. I'll help you make the best meal you can
24 put on your table. See past my bloody apron and know
25 there's a real brain behind this brawn. *Comprende?* OK,
26 who's next? What's your pleasure? Tenderloins or strip
27 steak? How thick should I cut it?

30. The Compassionate Soul

1   Once I remember my dad telling me to always put myself
2 in someone else's shoes. That advice has gone a long way. If
3 I see someone being bullied, you'll find me fussing at the
4 bully. Just letting him have it. I'm always rooting for the
5 underdog. It's my nature. I've always been that way. When I
6 see someone's eyes mist over, I get misty-eyed. If I noticed
7 someone crying, I have to pull them aside and ask them
8 what's wrong. Some people might look at it as a character
9 flaw. I don't see it that way. I feel like it's even better than a
10 cat with nine lives. If you care as much about other people
11 and their lives, it's like living their life, too. Feel their joy and
12 their pain. Feel their happiness and sorrow. In other words,
13 love them. I mean *really* love them. Not just the surface love
14 or superficial love, but the kind that lets them know that you
15 really care about what's going on in their lives and that you'd
16 do anything to help them. I see you tearing up. Is it something
17 I said, or is there something going on in your life that has you
18 upset? Tell me. I'm a good listener. I've been told that. I won't
19 tell a soul. I promise. See that girl over there? I can tell when
20 she's going to boo-hoo. The red starts working its way up her
21 neck. It's flushing, really. Then her cheeks get red and before
22 you know it, her eyes are red and wet. I've learned to
23 intervene when I see the red creep up her neck. It starts with
24 a smile and a friendly, "How's it going today?" When I have
25 her attention, I ask her if she's OK. Sometimes she'll open
26 up, sometimes not. She might even tell me what's wrong. If
27 I'm lucky the red will stop moving upwards and I might coax
28 a smile out. Ahhhh, I just got one out of you. That's
29 priceless!

31. The Crew Team Member

1   When they suggested that I join the crew team, I
2 thought they were crazy. I mean, who wants to show up at
3 school with frizzy hair? Getting up at four o'clock in the
4 morning should have been enough of a deterrent, but now,
5 I really wanted to earn that scholarship. What I didn't intend
6 to find out was how much it would change my life. Getting
7 up that early became a course in discipline. It made me go
8 to bed earlier, way before my friends did. I missed a lot of
9 the online gossip, and it made me get my homework done
10 earlier. It changed my life in so many ways. I'd show up at
11 the site where we joined to launch the kayak. Thankfully,
12 the members of the team were all morning people, or it
13 never would have flown. We had to learn to row in sync with
14 each other. There was none of that "I paddle faster than you
15 do" stuff. Everyone had to pull his weight so the workload
16 was even. It could be no other way. There was something
17 about breathing the morning air and watching the water
18 fowl. They seemed to know something that I didn't. Maybe
19 it was the peace I found in getting out before the ebb and
20 flow of traffic over the bridge nearby. I came to be
21 mesmerized by the rhythm of the water and the nature
22 around me. Frogs and fish became our friends as we cruised
23 through the shared waters. An occasional crabber would
24 buzz by and throw up a hand. Usually they had sense
25 enough to slow down. If they didn't, we'd rock on the waves
26 as we paddled. Smiling, we'd keep on rowing, one with the
27 river. There's nothing like it. Nothing. *(Looks down and lights*
28 *fade out.)*

32. The Docent

1   I might be retired, but I ain't dead yet. I wasn't sure what
2 I wanted to do with myself after leaving my job of forty years,
3 but here I am, a docent. One letter away from decent, it's a
4 pretty decent way to spend my time. I show little kids around
5 the marine science museum. There are sharks and stingrays
6 to look at. They are encouraged to touch some of the sea
7 animals, but some things are hands off. I have to watch out
8 for the little kids who like to wander off. We don't want to find
9 a surprise kid hiding somewhere when we're ready to lock up
10 at the end of the day. There are a lot of things to memorize
11 with this job. Compare it to being a waitress and having to
12 memorize the dessert list. While that's a sweet thing to do,
13 there's nothing sweet about being asked questions by
14 someone with a doctorate who knows a lot more about
15 marine biology than you do when you're a volunteer docent.
16 What I really want to tell them is, they don't pay me to know
17 that, but I hold my tongue. I still do research and don't like
18 to be left with egg on my face when I don't know the answer
19 to something. Sometimes I laugh it off and say, "OK, let's let
20 Mr. Sea Lion over here tell you." Then the crowd will laugh,
21 the doctor will look foolish, and someone can ask me
22 something simpler to answer. It all works out. I love it when
23 families come. It's such a treat for them. They're always
24 amazed by the amount of sea life that can be touched. Just
25 don't get in your head that you're going to touch an electric
26 eel. That's a real no-go. Some electrifying experiences are
27 fantastic. That wouldn't be one of them. OK, now I have to
28 give someone a tour. This tour is full; can you come back at
29 twelve?

33. The Auctioneer

1   I come from an unusual group. Not many people can do
2 what I do. I'm an auctioneer. Talking fast is a gift. Normally
3 I sound like anyone else, but once my adrenaline starts
4 pumping and the competition heats up, I talk faster and
5 faster. I think it's like a hypnotic spell. When the rhythm
6 starts, people lose all judgment and they start raising their
7 paddles to some pretty ludicrous prices. But hey, it's all
8 good. It can all be in the name of good competition. Most of
9 the time it's calm enough, but boy, have I seen some
10 scuffles break out! I once was raising the price, and a couple
11 of bidders got in a fisticuff way in the back. They had to call
12 in security. It was not pretty. And you know what they were
13 bidding on? A chamber pot. Imagine that. It was a chamber
14 pot. Not just your ordinary chamber pot, but one that was
15 used for royalty. It was funny. The way I see it, those people
16 put on pants one leg at a time, just like I do. But hey, to
17 each his own. So they got in a fight over this thing, and they
18 wound up running the price way beyond reason. It seemed
19 they were both trying to make a point. Maybe it wasn't so
20 much what the item was, but that each wanted to outdo the
21 other one. That chamber pot went for two thousand dollars.
22 The person who was selling it was smiling like a Cheshire
23 cat, and I couldn't help but snicker to myself. It was a night
24 to remember. You never know what will bring out the
25 fighting spirit in a bunch of bidders. It's worth going to see
26 even if you don't bid. My nickname for the experience is
27 "friendly fire." The winner of the spoils? I believe his name
28 was John ...

34. The Family Reunion

1   What is it about family reunions that drives you nuts?
2   Don't you hate it when Aunt Kathy pinches your cheeks?
3   How about when they use this condescending high-pitched
4   voice to ask you how you are? And forget the possibility of
5   ever remembering what everybody's name is. There's no
6   way they're going to pose everyone for a big family photo
7   and make it look good. And the odds of everyone showing
8   up in khakis with a blue shirt? Ain't gonna happen. The last
9   one I went to, they had this tug of war. My uncles forgot that
10 upper body strength in young guys is a force to be reckoned
11 with. Uncle Bob had rope burns on his hands as his souvenir
12 of the reunion. The rest of us carried home a plastic cup
13 with Jones written on the side of it. Where do all these
14 people come from? Well, I guess it's to be expected that
15 when the Jones family has a reunion, people will come out
16 of the woodwork. Shucks, the mere mention of it on
17 Facebook, and look out — everybody and his brother shows
18 up. On Facebook, Mabel Jones mentioned that she was
19 bringing some homemade chocolate meringue pie, and
20 Joneses that aren't even kin were showing up. Hey, who can
21 blame them? Her pie is to die for. Everything went well until
22 someone mentioned the fact that one of the cousins got
23 married last week. Those who weren't invited caused a big
24 ruckus, and it was all downhill from there. Were you invited?
25 How many Joneses do we have out there? Raise your hand.
26 **Were you invited?** *(Peers into the audience and pretends to talk*
27 *to someone.)* **No? You weren't? Sorry about that.** *(Shrugs and*
28 *runs Off-stage.)*

35. The Couple in Love

1   Don't you just love looking at couples in love? I won't
2 even call them new couples. Sometimes they've been
3 married for decades. You'll notice them by the way they hold
4 hands. One will hear music that touches his or her soul and
5 reach out and touch the other one. It can work either way.
6 It's not one-sided. If you see them when they're eating out,
7 they don't seem to have run out of things to talk about.
8 That's when you know that someone really did some
9 searching to find the right one. Because what it all boils
10 down to, when the body doesn't respond the same way
11 when it's old, the thing that's left is good conversation. If
12 you don't have that, you have nothing in the golden years.
13 Real love will touch the other person any time, day or night.
14 Real love will walk up and plant a deep, wet kiss on the
15 other person with no warning whatsoever. Real love won't
16 need a reason to show up with flowers. It will just happen.
17 Inside all of us lies a need to be appreciated. A need to be
18 surprised and caught up in the emotion of being and feeling
19 cherished. If that need isn't in you, then you're missing a
20 real part of life. A couple in love will shut off the TV, turn
21 and face each other, and talk. Not *at* each other but *with*
22 each other. Put the cell phone down. Get off the Internet.
23 Walk outside and hold hands with the person who shares
24 your life. Rekindle the fire. Make the other person feel
25 special. Be a couple in love. *(Gives self a big bear hug and*
26 *walks off the stage.)*

36. The Handshake

1   When I shook his hand, it felt like a dishrag. Now, I ask
2   you, is that any way to shake someone's hand? Something
3   in me wanted to grab him and say, "If you're worth your
4   weight in salt, you'll learn how to shake someone's hand
5   like you really mean it." I don't like some mealy little
6   handshake that conveys the message, "I'm inferior or afraid
7   of you." Buck up and give me a firm shake. Your future
8   might depend on it. Don't look at me like that. Some people
9   may have either landed or lost a job because of a
10   handshake. Turn to your neighbor now and shake his or her
11   hand. Let them tell you whether your shake is strong or not.
12   Don't get mad and don't get even, either. Just thank them
13   for letting you know where you stand. What I need to do is
14   go track down the last person whose handshake felt limp. I
15   need to tell them that if I work with them a while, I will whip
16   their handshake into shape. Shape up that shake. You hear
17   me? If I don't tell you, someone else will, and it's not going
18   to be pretty. The guy otherwise seemed to be pretty on the
19   ball. At the podium, he had just delivered a powerful
20   message. I came up expecting a handshake that reflected
21   the power I saw at the podium. It didn't happen. Dishrag
22   city. Come on now, guys. You can do better than that.
23   Especially you guys of the cloth. Work on it. Feel the spirit
24   and give me a firm handshake. *(Pretends to shake someone's*
25   *hand and buckles to the floor.)* Whoa, looks like you got a little
26   help from a higher source there. *(Laughs.)*

37. The Fire Extinguisher

1   It hung on the wall in the cafeteria for years. Unnoticed.
2   Unused. Well, thank goodness it was unused, otherwise
3   there would have to be a fire. The real fire was in her soul.
4   She was the scapegoat. The one everybody picked on. The
5   one who was made fun of. They always chose her last in P.E.
6   It humiliated her and hurt her self-esteem. This little ball of
7   revenge festered in her like a boil that needed to pop. One
8   day, she was bound to pop it. It was almost time for the
9   prom. She'd seen the list of who was going. All the hot girls
10   and guys who you'd drool over. No one had asked her. She
11   couldn't even think of anyone she'd like to ask. That was all
12   she heard them talk about. Of course, her table where she
13   sat alone was so close to the cool table that she could
14   overhear what was being said. It was usually about the prom
15   and all the details. Who was riding with whom in the
16   limousines. What kind of dress they were wearing. Where
17   the guys were planning to take them for dinner. She could
18   take it no longer. The day before the prom, she noticed that
19   for lunch they were having strawberry shortcake. That would
20   be perfect. No one was going to notice the fire extinguisher
21   missing for a few minutes. She slipped down into the
22   cafeteria early, and when the cafeteria ladies were taking a
23   break, she took the extinguisher over to the shortcakes.
24   Spraying the extinguisher, she topped each shortcake with
25   the white foam. It looked enticing. Soon she would
26   extinguish them. *It was a long time coming,* she thought.
27   So, my friends, what's the moral of this story? Always make
28   sure it's whipped cream. *(Takes whipped cream can, tilts head*
29   *back, sprays some in mouth, and walks off.)*

38. The Fossil Collector

1   There's something about collecting fossils. I don't quite
2   know how I got started. Maybe it was the arrowhead I found
3   at Granddaddy's farm. There was something so cool about
4   digging up an artifact. It made me curious about the
5   arrowhead and the people who used them. If you come to
6   my house, you'll find a collection of things that I've dug up.
7   Well, maybe they're not all fossils, but it's an interesting
8   collection anyway. The best piece I have so far is a
9   *Chesapecten jeffersonius.* It's the state fossil of Virginia.
10 They say that Thomas Jefferson named them. It's really a
11 fossilized scallop shell, around three million years old. I
12 can't imagine something being that old. Even the oldest
13 teacher fossil at school isn't that old. I look at this fossil in
14 amazement that something that old is still around. I
15 suppose the only reason these are still here is that the
16 oxygen wasn't near it to break it down. Now there's a weird
17 thought. If oxygen breaks things down and it's our life
18 source, isn't the thing that we need most also killing us? Do
19 I have warped thinking here? Am I on the right track? It's
20 like we need the sun to give us Vitamin D, but if we get too
21 much, it can give us skin cancer. It's like a mixed bag. And
22 so I look at this fossil and some others I have collected and
23 wonder how much of a fossil am I going to be to my
24 grandchildren and great-grandchildren. It's a weird thought,
25 and one that has me touching this fossil and considering the
26 possibilities. Me, a fossil? *(Pauses and thinks.)* **Nahhhh** ...
27 *(Walks Off-stage.)*

39. The Fireman

1   I know what you're thinking. You're wondering what kind
2   of fancy dishes we're cooking down there. I'm sure you've
3   seen the fire truck pulled up in front of the grocery store.
4   Sometimes we have time on our hands and the wheels start
5   turning about good recipes. Our station has a great kitchen.
6   I'm the one who does most of the cooking at the station.
7   Not that I'm boasting or anything. Once we had a cook-off
8   with the station four miles away. It was Four-Alarm Chili.
9   Excuse the pun, but it really was four-alarm. I told some of
10   the guys that it was hot, but I don't think they listened to
11   me. One of them is a mild kind of guy, and trust me, mild
12   is what he needs to eat. He ate some of that Four-Alarm and
13   his face turned this beet-red color. I thought we'd have to
14   use a fire extinguisher on him. His ears were even turning
15   red. The smoke alarm went off. No kidding, it really did. I'm
16   not sure what set that off, but maybe it was the smoke that
17   was rising from his collar. I was starting to wonder if he was
18   one of those people who spontaneously combust. Scary
19   thought. I'd have to use the hose on one of my own. Drop
20   by the fire station sometime. Maybe if you're lucky, I would
21   have just made some of my Four-Alarm Chili. Can you take
22   it? Have you got what it takes? A fireman needs to be able
23   to handle something hot. Maybe he couldn't take it. Like
24   they say, if you can't take the heat, stay out of the kitchen.
25   And this is a special kitchen. Enter at your own risk. We
26   might have to take a fire extinguisher to you. No joke.

40. The Clown

1   *(Enters dressed as a clown with a tear painted on each cheek.)*
2   I'm Bozo the Clown. Yeah, that's right. My clown parents
3   didn't have much of an imagination. I could have been
4   named a million names, but that's the one I got stuck with.
5   "The Tears of a Clown" must have been written about me. I
6   even paint tears on my face. I could be smiling and happy
7   but no one would know it because of these tears I paint on.
8   Someone once told me that they don't trust clowns because
9   you can't really see what their faces look like. But think
10   about it, how many people wear an invisible mask every
11   day? You don't know what someone is really thinking inside,
12   do you? Maybe they're having a bad day, but they have this
13   frozen smile plastered on. You can't tell what's going on
14   inside that head of theirs. I used to get asked to do a lot of
15   kids' parties, but since I started painting on these tears, I'm
16   not asked to go to as many. I guess the kids got upset by
17   the tears. I think, "What's the big deal?" How about if I
18   paint tears on their faces? Would they feel like they were in
19   good company? Maybe I should stand on my head; the tears
20   would just look like apostrophes. What do you think? Sound
21   like a good idea to you? I'd be multitasking. Being a clown
22   and an acrobat, all at the same time. They can call me
23   Ozob. That's Bozo backwards. How's that sound? Think
24   that'll fly? What's wrong? Why do you look scared? Don't
25   you like clowns? I'm sorry. These tears turned upside down
26   look like something else. Here, let me show you. I'm not
27   really sad. It's all a disguise. I'll even sing, "Don't Worry, Be
28   Happy" for you. Give me another chance.

41. The Alien

1   Take me to your leader. Shucks, forget that line. Take
2   me to your troublemaker. I'm an alien, and I want to know
3   what's really going on down here. I don't want to meet
4   someone who plays by the rules; let me meet somebody fun.
5   Someone who will show me the ropes of how to get more
6   bang for your buck on earth. On my planet, we've squeezed
7   the fun out of every single avenue known to aliens. I've
8   tweaked every game and activity until there's nothing new
9   under the sun, the moon, or any of the stars. I'm light years
10   ahead of you in terms of technology. Don't even try to
11   explain to me that you mere humans have advanced so far.
12   I knew how to take apart and put back together something
13   as simple as what you call a computer when I was two
14   weeks old. Think you're smart? Don't even go there. I'm
15   going to last longer than you because I'm short, and short
16   beings live longer. It's not as much stress on my heart. I am
17   good at taking in images because my eyes are so big.
18   Unknowingly to you, I'm standing here snapping pictures of
19   you with my eyes. These eyes of mine are also lenses to the
20   camera. Scary thought, huh? While my skin has a bluish
21   tone, I'm really warm. Why, even when a fire is really hot, it
22   turns blue. I study what I see before me and go back and
23   report. My leader expects a real rundown on what I see here.
24   What I'm seeing is a society that seems bent on
25   communicating with their thumbs, something unknown to
26   me. I don't even have thumbs. Their vehicles are primitive.
27   Aside from the aircraft, their cars don't even fly. The
28   transportation system is alien to me. They have so far to
29   come. Light years.

42. The Hug

1   All I wanted was a hug. Something so insignificant but
2 so huge to me. She had no idea how much it would mean.
3 It became something of an obsession. I sat through classes
4 just looking at the clock, hoping the bell would ring and I
5 would see her. One day, it happened. I was standing in the
6 hall with some guys and she came up behind me. Suddenly,
7 I felt these arms slide around my waist. Her chest was
8 pressed up against my back, and I was in heaven. She had
9 no idea how much of a rush I got. My dream had come true.
10 My dream girl had given me a hug. It was the best day of
11 my life. I looked over my shoulder at her and smiled. She
12 looked surprised. "I thought you were someone else," she
13 said. Suddenly my bubble burst and everything I dreamed of
14 disappeared in a flash. If only I hadn't heard her. Part of me
15 instantly wished that I'd been deaf. If only I hadn't heard her
16 say those words. Surely I hadn't just heard her say that she
17 thought I was someone else. Maybe she just said that to
18 explain away what she'd done so people wouldn't think her
19 so wild. That must have been it. She was just saying that
20 to cover up the fact that she'd apparently been overtaken
21 with lust for me. To cover up surprising me with that big hug
22 in front of God and everybody. My heart was pounding. My
23 frown turned into a smile. It could happen again, I told
24 myself. She was still standing there, looking at me. "No
25 problem," I said. And I reached out and hugged her back.
26 *(Gives self a big hug and walks off.)*

43. The Easter Bunny

1   *(Wears anything from bunny ears on a headband to a full-*
2   *fledged Easter bunny costume.)*
3   We've probably never met before. You see, I run a
4   clandestine operation. It's done in the cloak of darkness or at
5   the butt crack of dawn. I'm in and out of houses so fast it
6   would make your head spin. And spin it will after you eat all
7   those marshmallow-y gooey delicacies. If you like Peeps, I've
8   got your back. If you like Whoppers, you'll have a whopping
9   good time once you find your basket of delight. If jelly beans
10   are what float your boat, you've got 'em. I once had a run-in
11   with Santa Claus. He thought I was stealing his thunder. I
12   really wasn't. I tried to explain to him. You can't compare a
13   basket to a stocking. You really can't. When we finished
14   arguing, I was a real basket case. He was pulling up his black
15   stocking socks and fixing to leave. I'd been honored that he'd
16   paid a visit away from the North Pole in the dead of spring.
17   Actually, I was shocked. The reindeer were sweating bullets
18   and Rudolph's nose was so hot, it had actually turned white.
19   And all this because of some deep-rooted jealousy. "I'm not
20   trying to replace your holiday," I explained to him. "They're
21   both equally special holidays in their own way," I said. I saw
22   him writing on some naughty or nice list. I'm not sure what
23   side I was on. Let's just say that I could be getting coal next
24   year. I looked at my supply list and decided what he'd get in
25   his basket. This meant war. I know that sour things make him
26   wink. I found the sourest candy I could and put it in his basket.
27   Those eyes of his should be shut a really long time. Wow, did
28   I just say that? Hey, I mean no ill will. It's all good. He won't
29   mind. Besides, he's a jolly old soul. Right?

44. The Idealist

1   You can spot me in a crowd. I'm the one with the smile
2   on my face. They say fake it 'til you make it. That applies
3   to looking happy, too. Plant a smile on your face and see if
4   it turns your mood around. I dare you. In a utopian world,
5   everyone would have food to eat and a roof over their head.
6   Don't call me a Communist, and I'm not a socialist either. I
7   just think that everyone should have a fair share. It's only
8   right. Now that's not to say that people shouldn't work for
9   it. Those who work hard should get even more. It's like the
10 dessert after a meal. The icing on the cake. The cherry on
11 top. See that party over there? Ideally, everyone should go
12 home happy. What a great world that would be. Invariably
13 there will be one little girl who will go home jealous because
14 she wants something that the birthday girl got. It's human
15 nature. If you're an idealist, you go expecting to have a good
16 time and hoping to see everybody leave in a good mood. You
17 don't anticipate seeing Joey leave crying because he was
18 afraid of the clown. An idealist is often the peacemaker. I
19 hate seeing people who don't get along well with others.
20 Doesn't it suck to feel friction? To know that people aren't
21 getting along just makes everything more difficult. In an
22 ideal world, we'd all try to support each other and encourage
23 each other to do our best. And who doesn't want an ideal
24 world? One where a banana split has no calories and a work
25 day lasts four hours. Come to think of it, it's time for me to
26 clock out. See ya.

45. The Interview

1   (*Holds a sign that says "Finally a Grown-up" at his side.*)
2   I think it went well. The job interview, that is. Now my
3   heart can slow down. I had no idea that when I went in to
4   interview for that job, there would be a conference room and
5   twelve people sitting in there. Was I applying for President of
6   the United States? Was there really that much riding on their
7   decision? I wondered about the importance of that job and
8   considered whether or not I wanted to do something so
9   obviously crucial. And so I survived the interview. The next
10   week would be equally stressful. Every time the phone rang, I
11   lunged for it. Were they going to call me or not? I felt like a
12   jilted lover. Thinking back over the interview, I considered my
13   answers to some of their questions. What was my weakness?
14   I'd answered, "Not knowing how to say no. Putting too many
15   irons in the fire." They looked as though they were mulling
16   over my answer. What were my plans for the future? I hadn't
17   known how to answer that. It's not like I was ten with
18   someone asking me what I wanted to do when I grew up.
19   Although there are days when I wonder that myself. At what
20   point do you feel like you've grown up? When do you feel like
21   you've arrived? Somehow I don't remember ever taking the
22   interview of all interviews, the one that you take before some
23   age police decides whether or not you're officially a grown-up.
24   There seems to be a blurred line between adolescence and
25   being a grown-up. Some pass that interview and others never
26   make it there. I'm not sure when I had mine, but I will tell you
27   this, those age police don't cut you any slack. When you pass
28   those rites of passage, you'll know it. (*Walks out, wearing a*
29   *large sign that says "Finally a Grown-up."*)

46. The Inventor

1 People don't understand me. They think I'm weird. Let's
2 just say that I understand where Michelangelo was coming
3 from. He had notebook after notebook of inventions he had
4 dreamed up. How did these things come to him? I've often
5 wondered that. For me, they come to me when I'm in the
6 shower. You know how they make those shower crayons for
7 kids. Most mornings, you can find me standing in the
8 shower with those crayons in my hand, writing on the
9 shower wall. Hey, ideas can come and go like suds down the
10 drain if you don't write them down. The last time I had a
11 good idea for an invention, I spent an hour in there drawing
12 on the shower wall. The water was long gone. There I was,
13 getting chilled to the bone, when my boss called to ask
14 where I was. I was late for work. I got so caught up in the
15 design creation that I'd completely forgotten my game plan.
16 The designs were calling my name all day at work. When I
17 got home that day, I rushed to the shower but stopped dead
18 in my tracks when I saw that the shower was completely
19 clean. Later, my wife stopped me in the hall when she saw
20 this dazed look on my face. "Where are my invention
21 designs?" I asked her. She knew exactly what I was talking
22 about. "The cleaning lady came today. She usually comes
23 on Friday," she said. Anger boiled up in me like you
24 wouldn't believe. I was suddenly at war with Mr. Bubbles.
25 Mr. Bubbles had probably cost me a great invention. There
26 will be hell to pay, Mr. Bubbles! *(Walks off the stage with a fist*
27 *in the air. Someone blows bubbles at him.)*

47. The Baker

1   *(Has cell phone in his pocket.)*

2   If there's one thing I can't stand, it's the candlestick maker.

3 I mean, really. What kind of claim to fame is that? What a dip.

4 He acts like a wax dummy. So stiff. You know the rhyme: the

5 butcher, the baker, the candlestick maker? Well, the butcher

6 and I get along famously. He cuts right to the chase. No beating

7 around the bush with him. What you see is what you get. What

8 sheds a light on the fakeness of the candlestick maker is his

9 penchant for having to shine. No matter where he is, he has to

10 be top dog. It's unreal. I show up with my cupcakes, and he has

11 to pull this one-upmanship. He's got some chandelier thing

12 happening. Each one is bigger and brighter than the one before.

13 It's hard to top. How do I deal with that? If I show up with a

14 birthday cake, he's going to prove to me that his candles are the

15 best anywhere around. I'm at his mercy. Birthday time, I really

16 need him. I need to start a fad: birthday cakes without candles.

17 What else can we put on top of a cake? I mean, I want to break

18 this tradition, but I'm not sure how to follow that act. Burning

19 candles are a tough act to follow. I mean, everybody has the

20 urge to blow out their candles. It's like they think they're turning

21 back the hands of time with each puff. Maybe if I put sparklers

22 on top. Think that would make a splash? How about if we

23 bypass the whole candles thing? I know what I'll do. I'll use

24 some of those flameless candles. I'm sure that would go over

25 like a lead balloon. Then the only one I have to be in cahoots

26 with is the Energizer Bunny. Got his phone number? Maybe I

27 can work out a deal with him if I offer him some carrot cake.

28 Think that'll work? *(Leaves the stage, keying in a phone number on*

29 *a cell phone.)*

48. The Fitness Trainer

1   I knew you'd come back. They always do. I give 'em five
2 free sessions with their fitness center membership, and
3 they're hooked. The bad thing is, they don't want to pay me
4 for the next sessions. OK, I see that look on your face. The
5 one that tells me that money doesn't grow on trees. Well,
6 neither does a good body. Think about it. Do you think
7 Tarzan got his body just sitting around watching the sun
8 rise and set? Do you think Jane got off on seeing him blow
9 up like a hot air balloon? No, she liked seeing him just a-
10 swingin'. Hanging and reaching from vine to vine knocked
11 off some calories, I'm sure. Not that he had a lot of carbs
12 to eat, though. He was miles from Sara Lee, not that she
13 wouldn't have made a good neighbor. Like State Farm, I'm
14 sure she would have been the best neighbor around as long
15 as you don't pig out on too many cheesecakes. OK, back to
16 working out. I see your jaw tense up. Stop it. Stop it right
17 now. I'm only doing this for your own good. Now tell me,
18 when was the last time you came to the gym? Be honest.
19 'Fess up. If you pay us every month and don't come, it's
20 nothing in the world but paying fat tax. You heard me right:
21 *fat tax*. Do you want to be found guilty of paying fat tax?
22 Maybe it has a nice ring to it, but only to us. Cha-ching!
23 Cha-ching! That's the sound of coins, music to our ears. I'm
24 not supposed to let you know that, though. This is purely an
25 unselfish desire on my part for you to be the best you you
26 can be. I want to see you able to climb that mountain and
27 jump that stream. OK, I exaggerate a little. I'd at least like
28 to see you walk around Busch Gardens without losing your
29 breath.

49. The Phlebotomist

1   Could you roll up your sleeve, please? Just a little sting.
2   I promise it won't hurt much. I've been doing this for years.
3   Call me a vampire if you will. I'm the one who takes your
4   blood. The one who checks to see which vein is nice and
5   juicy-looking. The one who makes some people pass out on
6   the floor. I don't like it when that happens. I'm just doing
7   my job. Mind you, I try to behave myself and not have too
8   much fun doing this. At Halloween I've thought about
9   coming to work wearing fangs, but I think that would freak
10   people out too much. I could leave the medical jacket at
11   home and put on a black cape or something morbid like
12   that. Do you think that would cause a disruption? Create a
13   little extra interest down here at the lab? It would only be in
14   your best interest, of course. OK, which arm was it again?
15   Ah, yes, it's the one with the fat and juicy vein. Sorry if I'm
16   salivating. Oops, did I just say that? Sorry, I was thinking
17   out loud. And what's your blood type? If you're an O
18   negative, I'm going to pursue you like crazy. You have the
19   universal blood type. Did you know that? Don't be surprised
20   if your phone starts ringing off the hook once that gets out.
21   Oh, I'm sorry. I guess my job makes me a little overzealous
22   sometimes. OK, where were we? There you go. Ball up your
23   first. OK, release it now. Close your eyes for a minute. Just
24   a little stick. All better now?

50. The Lumberjack

1   Name's Ben, but you can call me Paul. You know, like
2 Paul Bunyan. I make my living chopping down trees. It's a
3 rough job, but somebody's gotta do it. My phone rings off
4 the hook after a big storm. You can find me out there
5 swinging away with an ax, just growing these muscles.
6 Would you like me to flex my arm? Hey, who am I kidding?
7 You've got me. I must confess, I tote a chainsaw like the
8 best of 'em. What, do you think I'm crazy? Sure, it's a
9 romantic notion to think we're still out there swinging axes
10 and looking all buff, but we have to put food on the table.
11 You can cut down only so many trees in a day's time with
12 old-school tools. Maybe the dudes down in Williamsburg
13 want to do things like they did back in the day, but I'm not
14 dressed in colonial attire, nor do I dance at a cotillion. This
15 is not to say that I'm not as manly as my ax-toting ancestor
16 now. There's still a lot of work involved with loading up all
17 those logs. I've got the arms and chest to prove it. The more
18 trees there are to cut down, the happier I am. When I see a
19 storm heading our way, I start counting the money. Uh-oh,
20 I guess that sounds greedy. Maybe I shouldn't talk that way.
21 Hmmmm. What's a better way to say this? This is all to
22 keep you safe. It's all purely for safety reasons. Remember
23 that the next time you give us a call. We'll be right there,
24 toting our axes ... I mean, chainsaws.

50
MONOLOGUES
FOR GIRLS

1. The Author

1   Just like a prize fighter, I have to have a strong hook.
2 You know ... to grab the reader. The person who's going to
3 stumble across my book in a library or bookstore. The
4 person I'm indirectly talking to. The person who, hopefully,
5 won't be able to put my book down for love or money. You
6 know the kind of books I'm talking about. The ones that
7 touch your life in ways that nothing else could. The books
8 that stay with you for years. Maybe even teach you a thing
9 or two. The ones that could even help you make decisions
10 later on. Who knows? How did I get this way? I mean, being
11 an author and all. I fell in love with words at an early age.
12 The ebb and flow, the rhythm and the power of words.
13 They're beautiful and poetic. They don't even have to rhyme.
14 Heck, just listening to some folks talk can set off my muse.
15 Try this sometime: go to the mall and pick a nice spot to
16 people watch. That's right, I said people watch. You're a fly
17 on the wall. Watch the way they interact. See how they talk
18 to each other. It's a study in human nature. Kind of like
19 what I do when I'm in a bookstore and I see someone pick
20 up one of my books. They first judge the cover. Next, they
21 flip it over and read the back and I'm thinking, but it's
22 what's inside that really matters. Yeah, of course the price
23 matters, too. We all gotta tighten our belts. Then I think
24 about my last name. Where is my book going to sit on the
25 bookshelf? Next to Stephanie Meyer or Walter Dean Myers?
26 Would it get more attention if my last name was Ridley and
27 I sat next to Rick Riordan?

2. The Cafeteria Lady

1   Hi, there. Nice to meet you. I'm the woman who dishes
2 out your food every day in the cafeteria. You know, the one
3 who puts those ice-cream-scoop-shaped mashed potatoes
4 and slabs of mystery meat on your plate. I can sling Chinese
5 food like the best of 'em and remind you to get some of our
6 great spicy ketchup, too. Yum. I'm actually part cafeteria
7 worker, part cop. I can spot someone trying to break in line
8 a mile away and nip it in the bud. All right, I see someone
9 trying to do it right now. You sir, weren't you supposed to
10 be in the back of the line? And just because you're cute
11 doesn't mean you get to parade yourself to the front of the
12 line. Get on back. Keep going, keep going. There, that's
13 better now. Anyway, like I said, I sling food like the best of
14 'em. Spaghetti and meatballs, got it, meat loaf, got it, fried
15 chicken, nope, wait a minute ... forget about fried. We're all
16 about being healthy now. That's why you're going to see lots
17 of green peas on your plate. If they're an especially bright
18 green, you can count on being able to also play marbles with
19 them later. Sorry, did I just say that? Sorry, Chef. I'll let you
20 play next time. Oh, back to work. What would you like on
21 your plate? A nice burrito? A slice of pizza? Some tofu? Hey,
22 quit breaking in line ... !

3. The Cake Maker

1   It all started because I wanted a decent-looking
2 Superman cake for my son's birthday, and now look at me.
3 I'm up to my elbows in cake batter. They just didn't have
4 good enough cakes down at the Food Tiger. What can I say?
5 I'm picky. So sue me. Nope, no good-lookin' Superman
6 cakes to be found. So what does this chick do? I roll up my
7 sleeves and get to work. Slinging flour and water and sugar
8 around 'til, goodness knows, I have some of the best cake
9 batter you've ever seen on this side of the Mississippi. Just
10 tell me what kind of cake design you want, and you've got
11 it. Want a cake that looks like a patent leather purse? You
12 got it. Want a cake that looks like a bottle of coke? You've
13 got it. Nothing is impossible here at Caitlin's Cakes. Need a
14 wedding cake that competes with the Empire State
15 Building? Not a problem. All right, so it might have thrown
16 me for a loop when those little girls started asking for
17 cupcakes on their wedding day. So it's not exactly how I
18 was brought up, but to each her own. And don't be thinking
19 that those cupcakes are mamby pamby. I can inject those
20 things with juices that'll have 'em all standing in their
21 chairs dancing, and we're not talking about fruitcake here.
22 And pastries, Lord, we've got pastries. No, I didn't say
23 pasties; get your mind *out* of the gutter, young man. This is
24 a clean-cut bakery, mind you. Now if you'll excuse me, I've
25 got some baking to do ...

4. The Candle Maker

1   You owe me a lot and one day I'm going to collect. How
2 dare I say such things to you, huh? That's right, you can
3 thank me for not being totally in the dark when the lights go
4 out. You know, those times when the power goes off for
5 some ungodly reason and you're left in the dark with nothing
6 but two hands to hold in front of your face that you can't
7 even see. When that happens, it's not exactly the time to go
8 digging around for candles. You'd better instinctively know
9 where those suckers are when that happens. Dripless is
10 preferable. I mean, if you can't even see, how are you going
11 to know if you're dripping wax everywhere? And do you
12 know how hard it is to scrape up dried-up wax? Not a fun
13 job. As far as picking candles goes, the sky is the limit. You
14 got fat ones, skinny ones, candles that float in water. You
15 got candles for birthday cakes, yeah there's some cruelty
16 there. I mean, what person who's turning eighty wants
17 eighty candles on their cake? That's job security for me and
18 a sure bet on a visit from the fire department. I'm just
19 sayin' ... We are so adored that homes even have shrines for
20 us. Haven't you ever seen someone's candle cabinet? The
21 place where candles either sit to be burned or they go there
22 to die. The candles with the black edges on the glass, the
23 ones that are too ugly to burn and too good to throw out.
24 What a mess. I've even seen other candles refuse to sit by
25 them. It's a sad sight, I tell ya. Do them a favor — use 'em
26 before they reach that point. Burn, baby, burn.

5. The Florist

1　　Oh, you caught me at a bad moment. Sorry, I don't have
2　time to talk. It's just that I have all these flowers to
3　arrange. It's the day before Valentine's Day, for crying out
4　loud! Can't you read a calendar? You really should have
5　come on another day. OK, whatever. Pull up a chair. I can
6　at least be hospitable. If I seem to ignore you, it's because
7　I'm up to the wazoo in roses and carnations. If I never see
8　anything else that's the color red, it will be all right with me.
9　And the smell ... I used to like the smell of roses, but now
10　it's making me gag. Kinda smells like old lady. Oh, sorry ...
11　I didn't mean it like that. Just sayin' ... My fingers are
12　bleeding from being pricked by thorns. And I wonder just
13　how many jerks are sending roses to girls who don't even
14　like them. I don't mean to be negative. I really don't. It's
15　just that ... well, Valentine's Day has its ups and downs. For
16　me, the up-side is more money from overtime. The down-
17　side is that I wind up with serious allergy problems by being
18　surrounded by the Botanical Garden contained in these four
19　walls and no time to spend with my own valentine. Well, if I
20　even had one. Who knows? Maybe one day I'll get lucky and
21　someone will send some red roses to me. What's that you
22　say? It's not supposed to work like that? Hey, we are an
23　equal opportunity flower sending company. Come on, guys,
24　make my day.

6. The Gardener

1   I can tell by the looks on your faces that you've never
2   dug up fresh potatoes. I kid you not. You just have that look
3   about yourselves. Have a little dirt under your fingernails?
4   That's a tell-tale sign of a potato digger. I grew up being like
5   this. I mean, loving potato digging. It's like panning for gold.
6   My sisters and I would have competitions to see who could
7   come up with the most spuds. We joked and called
8   ourselves the three spud-loving sisters from Idaho. Mom
9   always wanted to take those potatoes to cook and mash
10 them. Mash those little tater brains. Now I ask you ... is that
11 cruel or what? And to think what their fate was after I'd
12 bonded with them out there on that potato mound. I think
13 the most humane thing she could do is cook them whole in
14 the microwave where they'd cook from the inside out,
15 alleviating any pain they felt. Haven't you seen them
16 weeping from those eyes they have? It's cruel and unusual
17 punishment, I tell you. And French fries, don't even get me
18 started. Talk about being torn limb from limb, or eye from
19 eye, whatever the case may be. So the next time I'm at your
20 house and you offer me some creamed potatoes, don't think
21 I'm crazy if my eyes tear up. I'm just being empathetic.

7. The Goth

1   They say, "Don't judge a book by its cover." Case in
2 point ... look at me, for instance. My nails are black, so's
3 my lipstick. This blonde hair has been dyed a jet black and
4 my necklace is made of spikes. I might look really rough,
5 but when I'm at a tear-jerker movie, I can go through a
6 whole box of tissues. The one you have to look out for is that
7 cute little something in tiny floral print whose animosity
8 runs deep. You have no idea what goes on in her head 'til
9 *boom,* you're toast. Unlike me. Unless you know me, you
10 might steer clear, thinking I'm bad news, but nothing could
11 be further from the truth. Why, just yesterday I rescued a
12 kitten stuck in a tree. You can't get more warm and fuzzy
13 than that. Can you? That little ball of fur was just purring
14 away. It didn't judge me by these spikes and dark attire.
15 That little kitty thought I was the bomb for rescuing it. How
16 incredible is that? These gauged ears and the butterfly
17 tattoo on my arm are nothing but a form of self-expression.
18 They don't mean I'm the next woman on the most-wanted
19 list. My pierced eyebrows just show that I'm tough and can
20 endure anything, anything except maybe your negative
21 comments about my persona. The tattoos and piercings of
22 today are yesterday's leisure suits and bellbottoms. They're
23 just a sign of the times. And time is fleeting. If you'll excuse
24 me, I have an appointment with a tattoo artist. *Ciao.*

8. The Librarian

1   I know when you find out I'm a librarian, you'll
2 immediately talk in quiet tones. Well, what is that all about?
3 I like my library loud. Yell across the room, I don't care. The
4 way I see it, if it's fun in here, everybody will want to come
5 hang out. You never know what I'll do next. If it's your
6 birthday, count on me to bubble "Happy Birthday" with my
7 lips blowing into a glass of water. But first you'll think I'm
8 going to throw water on you. What a hoot. Then you were
9 fooled into thinking that we had a box of historic bones
10 shipped to the library. You should have seen your face when
11 I burst out of that cardboard box. If students come in to do
12 research, I hype them all up to think it's the coolest thing
13 to do since sliced bread. Waving at them at the door with
14 my big ol' Hamburger Helper gloves on, who can resist that?
15 What's that you say? You don't like reading books? I know
16 what'll fix that. There will be a contest and for every book
17 you read, you can enter your name. Read twenty books, and
18 your name goes in the pot twenty times. How's that sound?
19 We'll bribe you with a Starbucks gift certificate if you read.
20 It's a free raffle ticket. *Free.* Oh yeah, did I tell you that it's
21 *free?*

9. The Maid

1   I spend my days going from hotel room to hotel room.
2 Don't be getting any wicked ideas, now. I'm a maid. And no,
3 I'm not French. I'm Scandinavian. So anyway, like I said,
4 I'm a maid. They say that cleanliness is the next thing to
5 godliness. I go in rooms behind people and freshen them up
6 so they feel like every day is the first day in that room. I even
7 fold a point into the first piece on their toilet paper roll to
8 make things look fancy. And I make sure you have more of
9 those tiny little bars of soap so you can add to your
10 collection back home. If I'm working in a super nice place,
11 you might even find a piece of chocolate on your pillow.
12 Doesn't that rock? Fluffing pillows is one of my specialties.
13 I can play Michael Jackson's "Beat It" on my headset and
14 puff that pillow out like nobody's business. When I finish
15 making your bed covers look perfect, I lay that bed runner
16 across it. It's like a note that says, "Sherry was here and
17 she made your room look fabulous." Even though I notice
18 your stuff, I don't take it. Boy, they'd have my head on a
19 platter if I did that. Trust me; my job is more important than
20 taking your string of pearls or your nice-looking golf club.
21 Sometimes I fool myself into thinking that I'm Jennifer
22 Lopez and Prince Charming is right down the hall
23 somewhere. Hey, you never know, ladies. Now, excuse me
24 while I get back to work. That couple might come back to
25 the room any time now.

10. The Piano Recital

1   I knew this day would come. The scariest day of the
2 year. All these months of practicing piano and taking
3 lessons are now culminating in a recital. I can hardly get the
4 word out of my mouth. If only I had spent more time
5 listening to Mrs. Ousley and less time thinking about the
6 pink iced cookies she gave me each week. It's an atrocity, I
7 tell you. Nothing puts fear in my heart worse than the
8 recital. Everybody is lined up according to ability level. I'm
9 not the lowest on the totem pole, but I'm far from being on
10 top. Thank goodness I don't have to follow the cream of the
11 crop. Wow, I just said a poem. Aren't you impressed? So
12 anyway, when the recital comes, I am reminded that I do
13 indeed have a heartbeat. I wonder if anyone watching can
14 see my heart pounding out of my clothes. Ba-boom, ba-
15 boom, ba-boom. What a cardiac workout. Maybe if I
16 imagined this recital every day, I wouldn't even have to go
17 to the gym for cardio exercise. It's my fourth year taking
18 piano, and I keep wondering when I'm going to divorce the
19 ebonies and ivories. It's funny, when I sit down to play, I find
20 it relaxing, but the recital is anything but. It's as though
21 those pink cookies are coming back up in my throat. I
22 swallow hard and keep playing. Maybe this feeling will go
23 away if I'm lucky. Playing *Madame Butterfly*, I try to pray
24 away the butterflies in my stomach, but it doesn't work.
25 Mrs. Ousley used to say, "Imagine your audience naked." I
26 glance over my shoulder and lose my place on the keys. It's
27 all downhill from there. There are frozen smiles on their
28 faces. I feel their empathy and see the heart pounding on

1 the girl who comes after me. I mentally wish her luck and
2 take a deep breath. Phew, it's over until next year. Same
3 time, same place.

11. The Potter

1   I hold in my hand a piece of pottery. I call it an extension
2   of myself. Every curve, notch, and crevice is of my own
3   doing. Starting out with a lump of clay, I molded it as
4   though it were my child. I sent it to the kiln, hoping it
5   wouldn't crack in the heat. Like Hansel and Gretel thrown
6   into the oven, my baby went through the rites of passage. It
7   was green no more. Like changing from a child to an adult,
8   losing innocence along the way, it took the heat and stayed
9   intact. Look at me! I'm the proud mama of a crock. Will I
10 drop it and shatter it once it's arrived at its final state? Am
11 I that clumsy? And if it survives, what will I use it for?
12 Holding utensils in the kitchen? Holding brushes in the
13 bathroom? Maybe holding silk flowers on the kitchen table?
14 *Terra Cotta* is its name. Like earth, wind, and fire, it doesn't
15 get more basic than that. Ashes to ashes and dust to dust
16 runs through my mind. If *Terra Cotta* broke, would it shatter
17 to a powder to be swept up and tossed? Maybe one day to
18 filter down, be made into clay and reshaped again by
19 another potter? Are we all recycled? Are our souls just
20 drifting around watching the next potter who comes along
21 using the same clay over and over again? I clutch the pot to
22 my chest and decide to live in the moment. Nothing matters
23 but right now. Here, where I'm standing. Fingers touching
24 something solid. Something that matters to me and maybe
25 no one else. I close my eyes and feel myself become one
26 with it, my fingers become extensions of its curvy shape. It
27 breathes with me, changing from something inanimate to
28 something alive.

12. Alvin's Cousin

1   Hi. My name's Charlene, but you can call me Chip. If I
2 look beady-eyed to you, it's because I can spot a mighty fine
3 morsel from a mile away. What's that on your shoulder? A
4 potato chip crumb? Please, allow me. There's that's better.
5 Hmmmm. It's sour cream and onion, isn't it? Now, back to
6 the object of my lust. I have a wide-open heart for discarded
7 food. I consider it my duty to adopt any unattended food I
8 see lying around. Take the cafeteria floor at school, for
9 instance. You can find some good eats there. Slabs of
10 mystery meat. Vegetables such as turnips and rutabagas.
11 You know, fine food like that. My friends always pack extras
12 and have a big time passing their discards to me. It's
13 become something of a spectator sport. They call me Chip
14 Chomp. Allow me to explain my system. I have layers of
15 pockets in my cheeks. The appetizers go in the first layer of
16 pockets, followed by the main course, and the dessert goes
17 into the pockets located nearest the outside of my cheeks.
18 I've gotten it down to a science. I can save a slice of apple
19 pie from lunchtime to eat during sixth bell. The teachers
20 look at me in a strange way, but they never have the
21 courage to ask me if I'm eating anything. They can't see
22 food in my hands, so I guess they haven't figured it out. This
23 skill comes in handy when my sister, Darlene, turns her
24 head at the dinner table. Suddenly her dumplings are gone
25 in a heartbeat and no one's the wiser. I have one friend,
26 Camelia, who has learned the sport of layering food. We
27 never turn our backs on each other. When we sit together at
28 lunch, we sit three chairs apart. Soon we're going to see

1 who can make the most layers. But each of us gets to
2 decide what the other one will eat. I've already planned what
3 Camelia will be eating. The appetizer will be sauerkraut and
4 olives, followed by a main course of pig's feet, and a dessert
5 of scrapple pie. Come watch. It should be lots of fun. Well,
6 it was nice talking to you. I'll see you later. Wait a minute,
7 is that a crumb on your shirt?

13. High Fiber

1   My name's Monica, and I'm a wordaholic. I never meant
2   for this obsession to get out of hand, but somehow it did. It
3   all started with a fortune cookie. Most obsessions start
4   small. Anyway, this blasted cookie said I'd have financial
5   trouble in the near future. Now I ask you, what kind of
6   fortune is that? So I ate it. Not just the cookie, but the
7   stupid fortune along with it. It was a little rough going down,
8   but I managed. Felt kind of like one of those little fingernail-
9   like pieces of popcorn that gets between your teeth. That
10 was a step in the wrong direction. I really shouldn't have
11 done it. The aftertaste had an almond quality to it that I
12 found appealing. Before long I was hooked. Not just on
13 fortune cookies, but on any kind of written word. I graduated
14 to the comics page. You may not know it, but my favorite
15 cartoon cat tastes like an orange, and the round-headed guy
16 named Brown tastes strangely like peanuts. Before I knew
17 it, I was into heavy stuff like the business section and stock
18 listings. I liked to start the day with the sports section.
19 Usually twenty minutes after this quick breakfast, I could
20 feel the energy popping out all over. Well, the love affair with
21 newspapers was short-lived, and I was in deeper than I'd
22 even imagined. When I went to the library, I'd look at the
23 bestseller shelves and get all excited. As my obsession
24 grew, I needed more serious subject matter. Encyclopedias
25 had become my passion. Starting with the letter "A," I
26 worked my way down the alphabet. I wonder what's next.
27 What comes after encyclopedias? The World Atlas? The
28 almanac? Where does it stop?

14. Jagged Jasmine

1   They say that a gap between your two front teeth is
2   sexy. Whoa, baby, I must be drop-dead beautiful. This
3   business of special good looks didn't happen overnight. It
4   took years of tooth neglect. Way back in sixth grade,
5   Danielle Thomas had enough candy in our locker to choke a
6   camel. Kids came from halls all over school to catch falling
7   BB Bats and Sugar Daddies when Danielle opened the
8   locker. Her favorite stuff was kept in a safe on the top shelf
9   of the locker. She made me take an oath never to touch her
10 secret stash, and I never did. Until the end of the year. On
11 the last day of school, I caught Danielle flirting with my
12 boyfriend. I thought long and hard about how to get even.
13 Revenge would be sweet. I marched straight to our locker,
14 opened it, and reached for the safe. I felt the excitement
15 building. I shivered as I thought of all the forbidden goodies
16 locked inside. Nervously my trembling fingers worked the
17 combination. Three turns to the left to the letter "E," two
18 turns to the right to the letter "A," and one turn to the left
19 to the letter "T." I pulled out a brown bag and inspected its
20 contents. Scooping out a handful of red jawbreakers, I tilted
21 my head back and threw them into my mouth. Carefully
22 closing the safe, I relished the moment to come. As I bit
23 down on the round delicacies in my mouth, I felt my teeth
24 crack and shatter. I heard Danielle come up behind me and
25 I smiled in spite of the horrible pain. I kept my mouth shut
26 so she wouldn't see the broken teeth. Danielle smiled at me
27 and reached for the safe. Opening it, she reached for the
28 brown bag and asked, "Would you like to play with my
29 marbles?"

15. Rice Krispies

1   Last night, it got too quiet at home. Everybody plugged
2 into their computer. Ear buds rule and no one was talking.
3 We're becoming a nation of mutes. Have you noticed?
4 Thumbing text messages, have we lost the human element?
5 The urge to call and actually hear someone's voice? Letter
6 writing is long gone. Is it a lost art? Now there's only the
7 email or text message. No wonder paper mills are shutting
8 down. So much for pretty stationery. The kind that comes
9 in a nice box. Sometimes it even has a fragrance. Back in
10 the day, women sprayed their notes with the perfume they
11 wore. Can't send a scent in a text. Can't entice a guy with
12 the smell you wear through an email. Communication is
13 losing its romance. So anyway, back to the night before.
14 Like I said, it was way too quiet in the house. Even the dog
15 looked at me, wondering when I was going to talk to her. I
16 silently nodded and agreed with her. It was too quiet.
17 Looking for a little noise, I reached for a bowl. Smooth and
18 round. Empty and begging to be filled. In the pantry, I went
19 for the Rice Krispies. Snap, crackle, and pop. I lean my head
20 over the bowl of cereal splashed with milk and hear the
21 ruckus. It intensifies the closer I get to the bowl. The dog
22 looks at me in a weird way. A crispy piece actually splashes
23 a drop of milk at me, and I smile. It's way too much fun. My
24 black lab looks at me, wondering how something in a bowl
25 seems so alive. My cell phone rings, promising a voice on
26 the other end. Do I dive for it and risk eating soggy Krispies
27 or call them back? How hungry am I to hear a person's
28 voice? Starved for human interaction, I go for it. "Hello,

1 hang on a minute, will ya?" Munching on a spoonful, the
2 crackling continues. My friend on the other end hears it.
3 "Yep. You're right, it's good ol' snap, crackle, and pop. They
4 never let me down." And I laugh. My friend cackles, and I
5 accidentally drop the bowl to the floor, milk running
6 everywhere. Oh, snap.

16. Scales Go on a Fish

1   Yo. My name's Celeste. When summer comes you can
2 call me "See Less." I'll probably be sporting a swimsuit with
3 maximum coverage. Not like those chicks with their *gluteus*
4 *maximus* showing. I'm a real chicken of the sea. My fear of
5 showing skin started way back when in the splash pool.
6 Dixie and Susie always came over decked out in little
7 spotted bikinis, and I'd come strolling out of the house
8 wearing a tennis dress. A tennis outfit was difficult to swim
9 in, but it covered my body much better. When I was in the
10 Little Miss Bayou contest, I insisted on wearing a black
11 bodysuit instead of a swimsuit. It was my way or no way at
12 all. My obsession got worse. As I got older, I started wearing
13 jogging suits to the pool. That definitely drew a crowd and
14 before I knew it, it was a fad. Lots of girls were wearing
15 jogging suits until the lifeguard raised a stink. It made his
16 job too difficult. Not to mention the fact that he had a
17 harder time staying awake. One day, it occurred to me that
18 it was too hot in the summer to dress like an Eskimo. I
19 gradually worked my way down from a jogging suit to a skirt
20 and blouse, to shorts and a tank top. Finally, I made the big
21 breakthrough and bought a bathing suit. I had finally
22 relaxed at the pool when Susie and Vicky started all the diet
23 stuff. Here comes the clincher. You know what they have at
24 the pool? Vending machines. And do you know what is in
25 those vending machines? Exactly what you would be afraid
26 to eat in front of dieting friends. I don't want to be sewn up
27 in the sleeping bag and thrown to the bottom of the deep
28 end. To make matters worse, Vicky started bringing a set of

1   scales to the pool. Give me a break. What a place to have
2   such an instrument of torture. After giving it a lot of serious
3   thought, I decided what needed to be done with those
4   scales. Logical thought number one. Scales go on a fish.
5   Logical thought number two. Fish live in the ocean. Logical
6   thought number three. Relocate scales to proper area. The
7   rest is history.

17. I Want a Dog

1   Have you ever wanted something so bad you thought
2 you'd die if you didn't get it? Think back hard. Anything? Is
3 there anything you wanted that bad? For me, it's a dog. You
4 know the kind of dog that stares you in the eye, just
5 begging for you to take him home. There's no way I can let
6 him sit in that cage another day. OK, so I go home and
7 plead my case. I put on my own puppy dog eyes and pout
8 my lip like Mom does when she's talking Dad into letting her
9 buy some new furniture. Hey, it works for her, right?
10 Anyway, this dog could be the answer to my problems.
11 When boys tick me off, this dog will always be there, ready
12 to soak up my tears and love me unconditionally. That's
13 what I really need — unconditional love. The kind of love
14 that comes with a tail that's always wagging and that
15 friendly tongue just hanging out, waiting to lick me when I
16 get home. With a buddy like that, the whole world will seem
17 rosy. So I try to convince my dad that I really need this dog.
18 I told him that my grades will go up because I won't always
19 be going down the street looking for excitement. I tell him
20 that I'll do my chores and pick things up so the dog won't
21 chew on them. Then I tell him that it's either this dog or
22 riding lessons. I see the wheels turning in his head. He's
23 thinking riding lessons, horse boarding fees, equestrian
24 clothing, blah, blah, blah. He turns to me and says, "Which
25 pound is this dog at?" Bingo. I knew it would work. Gets
26 him every time. Yee-haw!

18. I Want a Prom Date

1   You there. Have you got a prom date yet? Don't look at
2 me like that. I'm not crazy. I'm just crazed. Crazed and
3 dazed because no one has asked me to the prom yet. What
4 I've doing now is asking guys instead of waiting for them to
5 ask me. What's that you say? It's not a good idea for me to
6 ask them out? Who died and made you Queen of Hearts? I
7 mean, where do you get off telling me that it's not a good
8 idea to ask guys out? Heck, just last week I had three guys
9 tell me they'd go with me to the prom. Oh, and now I
10 suppose you want to know why I bothered asking guy two
11 and guy three after guy one told me that yes, he'd go to the
12 prom with me? Well, guy two had a cooler car and guy three
13 has a cooler car *and* a great sense of humor. What's that
14 you say? What kind of guy is guy one? I'll ask him when he
15 gets off work. My brother's kind of busy these days. What's
16 that you say? You wonder why I'd ask my brother to the
17 prom? Oh no, you just heard me wrong. I'd never ask my
18 brother to the prom. That would be nuts. My brother, oh,
19 please ... no way. You have to be kidding. *(Phone rings.)*
20 Hello, Mom? No, Mom. You don't have to buy Rob a suit to
21 wear to the prom because he's not going. *(Hangs up phone.)*
22 OK, like I said, thing two and thing three, I mean guy two
23 and guy three showed interest, too. And the winner is, guy
24 two! Well, now that that's decided, it's time to look for a
25 dress, so if you'll excuse me — I have some serious
26 shopping to do.

19. I Want a New Hairstyle

1   I really need a new hairstyle. Desperate times call for
2 desperate measures. You see, this can make or break my
3 existence. It's crucial that I get my hair done, and it's
4 Monday. *Monday.* The shop I like to go to is closed on
5 Monday. How awful is that? If you need something done to
6 your hair and your favorite place is closed, you are so
7 screwed. It's awful! What am I going to do short of lopping
8 it off myself? I don't trust myself around a pair of scissors
9 tonight. Lord only knows what's going to happen once I get
10 home. Somebody call my mom please and tell her to hide
11 all the scissors and anything with a sharp blade. I'm
12 desperate. Anybody out there have a pair of scissors? This
13 is how I want it. See? I want it just above my shoulders so
14 it swings when I walk. Not too short. Not too long. But just
15 right. Like Goldilocks. You can even call me Goldilocks if
16 you want to. Just help me figure out how I can get my hair
17 done today since my favorite place is closed. I wonder if they
18 have someone on call. I mean, this is an emergency. It *really*
19 *is!*

20. The New Mom

1   I haven't slept for days. OK, maybe that was an
2 exaggeration. It just feels that way. Heck, where are my
3 manners? My name's Joy. Maybe right now it's a misnomer.
4 I'd feel more joyous if I got more than one hour's sleep at a
5 time. Nobody told me it would be like this. My bundle of joy
6 interrupts my sleep constantly. Gotta love 'em. When you
7 have a baby, count on not sleeping for a while. Like ever. I
8 used to be the biggest napper you'd ever want to meet. I
9 didn't need much of a reason to lie down and take a nap.
10 My feet hurt? Naptime. My head ached? Naptime. I worked
11 overtime? Naptime. Just for the heck of it? Naptime. Heck,
12 my middle name was Nap. I admit it. Anyway, back to the
13 bundle of joy. She's precious. She's the love of my life.
14 *(Looks Off-stage.)* OK, baby. I still love you, too.
15 Breastfeeding went well right off the bat. Or maybe I should
16 say right off the boob. The only thing is, nobody told me
17 that she'd want to nurse every hour. Who knew? All those
18 books I read, they didn't say anything about no sleep and
19 being a milk machine. I guess they knew that if they put
20 that in there, the population would suddenly come to a
21 screeching halt and there'd be no more babies born. Some
22 days are a real barrel of laughs. Ever seen a baby pee, poop,
23 and throw up at the same time? On you? There is no real
24 word to describe that. All I can say to that scenario is, you
25 gotta love 'em. OK, 'nuff about that. Have you seen my
26 darling baby's picture? What an angel. Come back. Come
27 back! I have two hundred more to show you ... *(Chases an*
28 *invisible someone off the stage.)*

21. The Novelist

1   Have chocolate, will write. That's my motto. I hear
2 people talk about their muse. My muse is named Hershey.
3 They say that dark chocolate is good for you. If that's so,
4 then I must be well on my way to great nutrition. If I'm
5 writing a scene and I'm stumped, I grab a handful of kisses
6 and my fingers move like lightning over the keyboard. It's
7 like magic. Have you ever tried it? Maybe it's the shape of
8 the delicacy. My tongue moves over the curvy shape and
9 something sparks in my brain. Something ignites that fire
10 that drives me to create. Once, I was stuck on a scene and
11 I was out of chocolate. It was an absolute crisis. The
12 characters were screaming for me to move the plot forward
13 and nothing was happening. I'd left one of them stuck in an
14 elevator with no way out. My muse was unattainable. Man,
15 that character was mad at me for days. The next day, I went
16 out and bought some chocolate and wrote the character out
17 of her catastrophe, but she never forgave me for it. Thus,
18 the next book was born, *The Chocolate Revenge*. It begat a
19 long line of chocolate titles. Yes, I can thank my muse for
20 that revelation, and a string of characters who have wished
21 me dead when I left them in precarious circumstances for a
22 day or two, or at least until I got to the store so I could get
23 my chocolate fix. I've tried carob to substitute, but it just
24 didn't work. My muse knew it was counterfeit, so it was
25 counterproductive. Think you can fool your muse? Think
26 again. Don't even try it. Now, it's time for me to sit down
27 and write, and there's something I need really bad. Anybody
28 got a candy bar?

22. The Prayer

1   *(A fork is in place On-stage.)*

2   Have you ever wished for something so hard you thought
3 you'd open your eyes and it would materialize? There is
4 something I've wished for so hard, I just knew it would be
5 there when I looked again. What was the object of my desire?
6 I'm going to string you along for a while and make you wonder.
7 Maybe you can guess what that might be. I have everything a
8 girl could ever ask for. I have great parents, a nice home, a
9 nice car, and super friends. I guess you can call me spoiled.
10 What else could make my life better? My grades aren't
11 suffering. I study enough. I'm in enough clubs to keep me
12 busy, so there's no lack there. On my birthday, my friends
13 remembered, and they gave me enough Starbucks cards to
14 keep me happy for a long time. So what could I need? What
15 was it that would make me smile? OK, I'll tell you. What I
16 wanted was an airline ticket. One that would take me to
17 England. My roots had been traced back to 1595 to Dorset,
18 England, and I wanted to go back there to see how it felt. I
19 learned about a hotel there that was owned by my eighth
20 great-grandfather, and it was still in operation. How cool is
21 that? Would I sense anything staying in the hotel? Would an
22 ancestor long gone whisper words of advice to me? On a
23 whim, I prayed in public and when I opened my eyes, there it
24 was. An airline ticket. I was standing in the food court at
25 McDonald's at the mall. When I looked down, there at my feet
26 was a ticket to London. I could hardly believe my eyes. This
27 was better than a Big Mac. Next I'll be ordering a burger at
28 Wimpy in England, where you eat a burger with a fork. *(Holds*
29 *a fork in her hand and yells, "Yes!")*

23. The Ring

1   This woman I know has this uncanny ability to guess who
2 it is that's calling her. Now, I'm not talking about the cell
3 phone. I know we use different ringtones to let us know who
4 is calling. I'm talking about the land line. Without looking at
5 the caller ID, she has this ESP that clues her in to who's on
6 the phone. At least she's given a series of three rings when
7 it's a solicitor. The bad thing is, sometimes people she
8 actually wants to talk to are on the other end, and she's
9 already decided it's a solicitor and chooses not to answer it.
10 One day, the call had a series of four rings. This was quite
11 unusual, and she wasn't sure what to make of it. She let it
12 ring and didn't answer it. She went to the caller ID to see who
13 it might have been. It said heaven. Well, that blew her away.
14 Since when did God have a phone? Sure, strange things had
15 happened to her with the phone before. She'd brushed it
16 aside but it came back to mind now and then. Once, she
17 needed to order some contacts but didn't want to spend the
18 money. The phone had rung. Someone on the other end said,
19 "Family Eye Care." She told them, "I didn't call you." The
20 voice on the other end said, "I didn't call you either." She
21 knew in her heart that someone bigger than her had
22 orchestrated that call so she'd order those contacts. Now,
23 she looked at caller ID and decided that next time she'd
24 answer the call with the four rings. An hour later, the phone
25 rang. It had a series of four short rings. After the second set
26 of four rings, she snatched it up and said, "Hello." She heard
27 a harp playing. Then it occurred to her. God is good at
28 technology. If God makes man in his own image and there are
29 geeks, God can be geeky too. *Wow*.

24. The Scent

1   In my hands, I hold a rose. A rose is a rose is a rose.
2   And a smell by any other name is not a rose. I used to think
3   that roses smelled like old lady. I have come to decide that
4   I am wrong. When I was walking by a rose garden with my
5   boyfriend and he got super excited, I decided that maybe
6   rose cologne was the way to go. And so I went to the mall.
7   Looking for a rose scent, I tried the makeup counter. There
8   were so many samples to try and this little strip of paper to
9   spray them on. After the sixth sample, my nose got
10 confused. I guess you could say that my olfactory zone
11 never *rose* to the occasion. I never found a rose perfume to
12 my satisfaction. What would work next? The next party we
13 went to, I took notice of the women wearing a pleasant
14 scent and studied the reaction of my guy's face as they
15 walked by. The scents that registered the most pleasure
16 were musky and jasmine. OK, so I had something else to
17 work with. Going back to the mall, armed with that
18 knowledge, I again braved the makeup counter. I sniffed a
19 number of musky scents and went home wearing the one
20 that said, "Come hither." Was it going to work? Was my man
21 going to jump up out of his chair and give me a hug? Just
22 as I walked in, the phone rang. He jumped up out of his
23 chair, but I couldn't tell if it was the come-hither perfume or
24 to answer the phone. He saw the look on my face, and his
25 decision making skills could stop on a dime. Giving me a
26 hug, he said, "You smell good." I wasn't sure if he was
27 trying to dig himself out of the hole he was in because I
28 realized he was going for the phone first, or not. I guess he
29 rose to the occasion after all. *(Laughs and heads off the stage.)*

25. The Séance

1   *(Place a flashlight On-stage beforehand.)*

2   Have you ever missed a relative and wanted to contact
3 them in the great beyond? Maybe asked them to give you a
4 sign if they could? Maybe knock three times or something
5 like that? Well, I'm here to tell you that maybe that's not a
6 good idea. This is how it went. My cousins and I decided we
7 would try to reach out to our Great Uncle Benny. Why Uncle
8 Benny? I really have no idea. I never even met the man.
9 Anyway, we were going to hold a séance. Now, before you
10 get all weird, we're not a bunch of witches, nor are we in
11 some cult. Our curiosity just got the best of us, and later
12 we wished it hadn't. Sitting in a circle holding hands, we lit
13 a flame and told him that if he was around, to let us know.
14 I held my breath and anticipated his response. Sitting there,
15 we stared at the flame, waiting expectantly. A few minutes
16 later, the flame grew really big and our eyes got just as
17 large. This was scary stuff. What's that you say? You're
18 asking me what happened next? Well, I'll tell you. We blew
19 out that candle so fast it would make your head spin. We
20 put the candle back from wherever we'd borrowed it and
21 went running out of there, never to hold a séance again. If
22 you get the urge to contact someone who's long gone, don't
23 do it. Go watch a horror movie instead. At least you can
24 leave the theatre knowing it was just on the screen. *(Shines*
25 *a flashlight under her own chin and laughs a wicked laugh.)*

26. The Seashell

1   *(Holds a large shell in her hand. A crab shell is placed On-stage.)*
2   In my hand I held the perfect seashell. It took me a long
3   time to find it. Many walks on the beach. Many years by the
4   shore. Many trips scouring the beach looking for just the
5   right one. I finally found it. Cradling it in my hand, I marveled
6   at its perfect shape. The smoothness on the inside and the
7   wavy and nubby texture on the outside. I held it to my ears
8   and listened. It spoke of rolling tides and thunderstorms. It
9   spoke of sailors who never made it home and mermaids who
10   splash between the waves. I became enchanted with its
11   spell and wanted to be sucked in. To become part of the
12   power from which it came. Listening to the shell, I walked
13   closer to the beach. One with nature, I entrenched myself in
14   the sand and let the waves wash over me. I stood in one
15   spot for a long time, charmed by the seagulls that flew
16   overhead and taking in the salty air. Putting it to the other
17   ear, it had a slightly different sound. I heard something
18   totally unexpected. A voice said, "Come to Bob's Crab
19   Shack." I pulled it away from my head. Was I dreaming?
20   Could it really have said that? About that time, a plane flew
21   overhead with the banner, "Come to Bob's Crab Shack."
22   Staring at the shell, I wondered. How could it have made
23   such a sound? Looking into it, I saw some kind of chip.
24   Maybe a motion sensor. The perfect shell had become the
25   perfect ad. Commercialism invading Mother Nature. The
26   wild thing is ... it worked. Guess who found herself eating
27   crab that night? Yours truly. *(Walks out listening to the shell*
28   *and holding a large crab shell.)*

27. The Supermom

1   I like to think of myself as everybody's mom. If you see
2 me at the bus stop and you aren't wearing a jacket and it's
3 cold, I'll ask you where your coat is. I can't help it. It's just
4 the way I am. Some people think I'm obsessive. When my
5 kids have homework, I'm on their backs like crazy. Forget
6 to do your assignment, and I'm your worst nightmare. And
7 don't even think you're going to get away with anything if I
8 show up in your classroom subbing. I know all the tricks
9 and have heard all the excuses. After all, I'm a supermom.
10 Being a supermom takes many skills. You have to be a
11 nutritionist. If your kid is going to eat the right foods, you
12 have to be armed with all kinds of nutrition knowledge that
13 only comes from studying books on health. I stagger into
14 the grocery store with notes and lists, taking time to
15 carefully read all the ingredient labels to make sure my kids
16 aren't eating too many preservatives and artificial
17 ingredients. I try to get my kids involved in sports and
18 activities that make them exercise their brains. Critical
19 thinking skills are important, especially now that every state
20 has students taking tests that rely on remembering a lot of
21 facts. I drive my kids to every conceivable museum or
22 gallery, grill them on area historical facts, and have them
23 listen to books on tape even as they sleep. What if they
24 learn to speak French in their sleep? Wouldn't that be
25 divine? I will leave no stone unturned in making sure they
26 are perfection in every way. Sure, they may be unpolished
27 gems, waiting to shine. Even in spite of whatever flaw or
28 handicap they have, I try to make them be their best
29 possible selves, because ... I am Supermom!

28. The Wedding Planner

1   When I wasn't looking, somebody made me a wedding
2 planner. I'm not quite sure how it happened. A friend of
3 mine was engaged and she was all thumbs when it came to
4 details. "I can't keep everything straight," she told me.
5 Problem was, she told me when we were out shoe shopping.
6 All I could think about that day was this perfect pair of
7 wedge shoes. They were to die for. I mean, these were shoes
8 that were cute enough to make you trade your baby brother
9 for them. The kind of shoes that stop traffic. The kind that
10 make you go to the head of the class. I'm just sayin'.
11 Anyway, I was so distracted by those shoes that when she
12 asked me if I'd be her wedding planner, I said yes. She could
13 have asked me if I could drive her to the moon and I would
14 have said yes. All I had on my mind were the shoes ... oh,
15 and maybe the steamed crabs we were going to eat next.
16 Now, nothing can compete with new shoes and steamed
17 crabs. Am I right? Do I hear an amen? OK, so I'm a wedding
18 planner now. What does that entail, you ask? Well, I have to
19 organize everything like when the flowers should arrive. We
20 don't want any limp and fading flowers there, now, do we? I
21 have to make sure all the attendants and escorts have
22 everything they need. The last wedding I planned, there were
23 eight attendants and eight escorts. Now that means sixteen
24 young folks to chase around. Some were prone to lose
25 shoes. Others lost their matching jewelry. I have to be the
26 brain that's walking around outside of their body for a few
27 hours that day. It's OK, I can take it. Maybe this job will
28 grow on me after a while. Maybe. What's that you say?
29 You're engaged? Hey, let's talk!

29. The Beach Cottage

1   Won't you come in? This is our home away from home,
2   the beach cottage. We've stayed here every summer ever
3   since I was born. See that chair rung over there? I cut my
4   teeth on it. Hey, I didn't know I wasn't the dog. I remember
5   barely being able to see over the window ledge and watching
6   the big girls and boys running down to the water with their
7   surfboards. Little did I know that one day I'd be one of those
8   surfer girls, too. It would scare my mom to death seeing me
9   out there, but she's always been afraid to let me have a
10 really good time. "Watch out, you're going to hurt yourself,"
11 she'd say to me. I'd look over my shoulder and smile at her
12 while I plunged headfirst into a big wave. We've had a good
13 time in this cottage. I remember catching fireflies in the
14 back yard. I got my first real bad sunburn one summer, and
15 I also got my first boyfriend here. I was thirteen. He was
16 fifteen. Yeah, that's right. Go ahead and admire me. I can
17 take it. I remember Mom rolling her eyes when she saw me
18 down the street talking to that boy. He was two whole years
19 older than me. I sigh just thinking about it. It was a
20 summer to remember. Lots of good memories in this old
21 beach cottage. The good memories help chase away the
22 bad. Like when someone broke into our home while we were
23 down here on vacation. Then the time the battery died in our
24 van. Then there was also the summer that the hurricane
25 messed up half our week here. Mostly, though, I get a happy
26 feeling just thinking about this place. I always hate to leave
27 it. It's like losing that boyfriend all over again. *(Looks down,*
28 *lights fade out.)*

30. The Attraction

1   It started innocently enough. I'd always loved that chair.
2 When I was a little girl, there was this chair down at the ice
3 cream shop with the metal curved back that I'd slide my
4 hand across as I licked the cold concoction. The charm of
5 going to that ice cream shop was the treat that lay ahead
6 for my tongue and the touch of that cool, curvy chair. My
7 parents noticed that I loved the chair and found one like it
8 for my room. Since the seat of it was a simple round
9 cushion, I changed the cover a few times a year. When I was
10 little, the material was pink and furry. As I got older, I
11 changed it to red leather. Then, my wild self changed it to a
12 zebra print. It went with the black paint I'd slapped on my
13 walls. I was feeling in a goth mood. Then one day it hit me.
14 I'd fallen in love with the chair. I'd heard of attractions to
15 inanimate objects before and scoffed the notion. Some
16 people fall in love with their phone. For others, it's
17 something weird like a stairway. For me, it was this chair.
18 Soon I had to start taking it places with me. If I went to a
19 concert outside, other folks might show up with those
20 foldable canvas chairs. I'd have that ice cream shop chair
21 with the zebra print seat. Guys came up to ask me if I'd like
22 to go for a walk at the concert, and I'd longingly look back
23 at the chair. "What's up with the chair?" they'd ask. I'd
24 shrug and laugh a little. Even I couldn't figure it out. It all
25 went well until one day I had to book a flight. The real fight
26 started when I tried to pass it off as a carry-on. They finally
27 let me leave it in the bathroom. It really causes me trouble
28 sometimes. *Help me!* Know any addiction groups out there
29 for this? *(Throws up hands and walks Off-stage.)*

31. The Beanie Baby Collector

1   *(Holds ostrich Beanie Baby. If an ostrich is not available, choose*
2   *another Beanie baby and customize the monologue to fit.)*
3   I have a room dedicated to Beanie Babies. You think I'm
4   kidding, don't you? They're compact, cute, and cuddly. Three
5   C's that are very important in a collectible. It started about
6   fifteen years ago. The company had the smartest marketing
7   plan ever. Create a cute product that started out with its own
8   self-made demand. Who could do better than that? I mean,
9   think about it. When these things came out, they instantly
10   increased in value. Wouldn't it be great if that happened to
11   your car when you bought it and drove it off the lot? Could it
12   get any better than that? Let me ask Stretch, my Beanie Baby
13   ostrich. Stretch was a gift from a friend at an art gallery.
14   Handing me the adorable ostrich, she told me that Stretch
15   was intelligent. "Just what I needed," I thought, and I happily
16   took her token of friendship. Stretch wore a furry collar. Just
17   looking at it gave me a warm fuzzy. And then there was this
18   little brown bear that was the first one I bought. That was
19   many moons ago. It was small enough that it wouldn't take up
20   much room. I bought it thinking, "What the hay, it's just a few
21   bucks and it's a nice collector's item." Little did I know that
22   I'd collect enough over time to fill up an entire room. So now
23   it's come down to this. At Christmas, I'm giving them away.
24   It's not re-gifting, it's repurposing. Some of these lovelies were
25   gifts from others. I figure, share the wealth. And the Beanie
26   Babies will love you for it. Why let them suffer in a box in the
27   attic when they can have a new home? Right, Stretch? Right?
28   *(Talks to a Beanie Baby and walks away, shaking her head.)*

32. The Beautician

1   Where did I put the flat iron? Have you seen it? Why do
2   those things always walk off? Do you have any idea how
3   much a really good one costs? We're talking big bucks here.
4   I'm not kidding. Those take the crimps out of your hair like
5   nothing else can. I spend eight or more hours of the day on
6   my feet. There's no wonder I need a pedicure once a week.
7   It's pitiful what these poor things have to tolerate. Being a
8   beautician, I'm also part psychiatrist. I know more about my
9   clients than their own spouses do. Every time they come in,
10   it's like a continuing saga on a soap opera. The stuff they
11   tell when I'm foiling, highlighting, cutting, and spraying their
12   hair, you wouldn't believe. I wouldn't trade this job for the
13   world. They're entrusting so much to me, not only their
14   beauty, but the keeping of their secrets, too. If they come in
15   and see me just starting work on another client, I see their
16   faces fall a little. They know that they don't have me to
17   themselves. You're smiling out there, aren't you? You know
18   it's true. It's true, isn't it? We all want to think we have our
19   hairdresser, nail person, or massage therapist to ourselves,
20   don't we? It's only human nature. Hey, even the dog claimed
21   ownership the other night. I was sitting on the deck in a
22   chair opposite my husband when I told my husband, who
23   was sitting on a double settee, that I'd come sit by him. The
24   dog was sitting by him on it and as soon as I said that, the
25   dog rested her head in his lap as if to mark her territory.
26   We're all territorial, from the pets in your house to yourself.
27   It only comes natural. Now if you'll excuse me, there's
28   someone coming in to get her hair done. She's someone

1   **who wants my undivided attention. Well, good morning,**
2   **Suzanne. I've been waiting for you.** *(Turns and looks away to*
3   *an imaginary person coming up.)*

33. The Diva

1   They hate me 'cause I'm beautiful. What can I say? I'm
2 a natural beauty. Hey, who am I fooling? I get up at the butt
3 crack of dawn to look like this. I have to exfoliate, mask,
4 and moisturize. I have pores to tighten and follicles to tame.
5 This long hair takes forever to dry, and I break out in a
6 sweat every time I pull out the blow dryer. Only my
7 hairdresser knows how much time and money is spent on
8 these tresses. If I go to someone different, heaven knows
9 what kind of cut and color I end up with. Ever seen bangs
10 at the back of someone's head? Well, neither have I. I just
11 wanted to make sure you were listening. And these nails?
12 You don't think I was born this way, do you? It takes hours
13 sitting there getting my hands and feet done. Nothing
14 comes easy. If I could do it myself I would, but why bother
15 when someone else is so good at it? I have to pay attention
16 to every detail from my head to my feet. Picking my clothes
17 out the night before, everything has to match. My jewelry,
18 my shoes, the right colors for my clothing. If one thing is out
19 of whack, it's all messed up. If I can't find the right shoes,
20 I have to go back to square one and start over. It's
21 maddening. You can pick me out in a crowd. I'm the one
22 who falls back at the mall when I see a big mirror. I have to
23 make sure everything looks good. I'm checking my hair, my
24 lipstick, and making sure I don't have anything green stuck
25 between my teeth. Being beautiful — it's a tough job, but
26 somebody's gotta do it.

34. The Diagnosis

1　By the way he held the clipboard, I knew it was bad news.
2　Usually doctors come in and just routinely lay down the
3　clipboard and start joking around about something. Maybe I
4　have the kind of face that says, "Joke with me." It seems to
5　work that way with my husband. Well, actually he tells me
6　that I have gullible written all over my face. Anyway, so the
7　doctor held this clipboard in such a way that it looked like he
8　really meant business. I knew that my diet wasn't the best in
9　the world. My cholesterol was up, but I was on medication to
10　bring the numbers down. My sugar level had been elevated
11　two out of three times, so that was something to watch. I
12　wondered what he was going to say and I held my breath. The
13　next words out of his mouth took me by surprise. He looked
14　at me and said, "I won the lottery." This was totally not
15　something I had planned to hear. "What did you say?" I
16　wanted him to repeat those words. He repeated it. "I won the
17　lottery." There, that confirmed it. "I'm giving up my practice
18　tomorrow." I looked at him in a state of disbelief. And all this
19　time I had worried that something was wrong with me. Now I
20　felt like something was wrong with him. How could he walk
21　out on patients who depended on him? I'd bared my soul to
22　this man. He knew so much about me and I trusted him with
23　my health issues. Now he was going to walk out of my life.
24　"But you took the oath," I said. "The one to help heal
25　people." He looked at me and laughed. He told me there was
26　nothing in that oath that said you can't buy a lottery ticket. I
27　had to get a grip on myself. At least he didn't give me some
28　terminal diagnosis. He was just going to be terminally rich. I
29　can live with that.

35. I Love Bling

1   What is it about bling? Maybe it's the way it reflects
2   light. Maybe it's the way it makes me feel like a queen. I
3   could be walking out to the trashcan, but put on the right
4   necklace, and *voila,* instant glam. Just check my jewelry
5   box and you'll find more bangles and baubles than you can
6   imagine. If you lined up all my necklaces, it would probably
7   rival the length of the Great Wall of China, and you can see
8   that from the *moon.* No kidding. I just love shiny stuff. I like
9   having tops that sparkle and shine when I walk. If you're on
10 a stage, it's all the better. But if you're acting in a film, they
11 really don't want you wearing anything like that. It could
12 pick up the light and sparkle, attracting the attention away
13 from the star actor they've flown in from New York and onto
14 you, a mere walk-on who's only earning one hundred dollars
15 a day. I have so much bling in my closet that I had to stop
16 and wonder just what was I going to wear when I went to
17 see my friend's baby. I mean, what baby is going to want to
18 snuggle up to bling? It not only scratches, it could cut that
19 little face. And so I find myself ditching the bling in favor of
20 something smooth. Something soft, like a baby's butt. But
21 I know when I return home, that bling is coming back out.
22 Maybe my friend will even teach her little one to dress in
23 bling. She'll be the cutest thing on the playground. It's
24 inevitable that this diva will bring up my own little darlin' to
25 love bling one day. Hey, wait a minute. I see some bling out
26 there. Shine the spotlight a little more in that direction.
27 Girlfriend, you really got it going on!

36. The Cliffhanger

1   If there's one thing I love, love, love in a book, it's a
2 cliffhanger. You know, the thing that keeps you turning
3 pages, chapter after chapter? Just when you think your eyes
4 are going to close on you, you read something that has you
5 sitting on the edge of your seat. Something that makes you
6 want to read more. It's amazing, really. How an author can
7 hold us spellbound like that. It happened to me when I was
8 reading an old Kathleen Woodiwiss novel. OK, so I'm a
9 romantic at heart. I couldn't put down that novel for
10 anything. I missed sleep to read it. Gave up meals to read
11 it. I didn't even answer my cell phone because I was reading
12 it. Now that is the sign of a good book. One that you can't
13 put down. It's the makings of a book that you'll carry with
14 you forever mentally. And now I go looking for that fix. Just
15 the book to make me forget that the rest of the world is
16 around me. One that will make me forget my own name and
17 where I live. One that will make me so caught up in it that
18 I am one with the page. I become the character and the
19 character is me. There is no dividing line. I meld with the
20 page. Now that is a good book. I know as early as the first
21 page. If it doesn't happen then, it's not going to happen for
22 me. It's like an early addiction. Something that grabs me
23 right away. Because something inside of me needs it. The
24 hook and the cliffhanger. Then the climax comes and makes
25 everything right. I take a deep sigh. It was all worth it. The
26 roller coaster ride comes to a stop, and I don't want to get
27 off. Ever. *(Lights fade out.)*

37. The Hopeless Romantic

1   Well, hello there. My name's Carrie. You can call me a
2 hopeless romantic. You can pick me out of a crowd by the
3 loose tendrils in my hair, the soft pink lipstick, and the
4 gleam in my eye when I see a couple holding hands. I've
5 always been in love with love. I can't help it. I like satin
6 sheets and musky perfume. I love romance novels and a
7 walk in the park. There's something about a macho man
8 holding a baby that really makes me all gooey eyed. It must
9 be the hint of sensitivity that shows through the tough
10 exterior. It almost gives me goose bumps to think about it.
11 Romantic movies put me in a tailspin. I watch the way
12 couples on the big screen glance at each other. Each knows
13 what the other wants or needs without even saying a word.
14 It's almost hypnotic. It makes me want to put pen to paper.
15 Something inside of me says, "Go with the flow baby, go
16 with the flow." It must be an adrenaline rush that kicks in
17 when I see two souls connecting on a spiritual level,
18 knowing that they're really into each other. There's nothing
19 better. All the riches in the world, all the big houses, all the
20 fancy cars, all the big titles don't hold a candle to the feeling
21 you get when you are on the same wavelength with someone
22 who has the same needs as you. And so I ramble and my
23 eyes travel from couple to couple, looking to see if they have
24 that special something. That spark in their eyes only for
25 each other that says, "There is no one on earth like you."
26 That "Every day I love you more." And so my search
27 continues. I must find it for myself. That spark I see in their
28 eyes. The one that satiates and drives them to passion. And
29 I will, because I ... am a hopeless romantic.

38. The First Bite

1   There's nothing like the first bite. I'm talking about the
2 first bite of anything. The first bite of watermelon. The first
3 bite of a piece of steak. The first bite of a brownie. It's kind
4 of like the first trip to a new amusement park. Everything is
5 so fresh and new to you. It's exciting. It doesn't get much
6 better than that. And so I held it in my hand. The Three
7 Musketeers bar. Anticipating the first bite, my teeth
8 hovered over that tasty chocolate, anticipating the whipped
9 chocolate that lay beneath. The phone rang. Of all the worst
10 times for the phone to ring. That first bite was so close, and
11 yet, so far away. Darn. I answered the phone. I probably
12 sounded short to the person on the other end. And no, I
13 don't mean Napoleon Bonaparte short, I mean short-
14 tempered. By their reaction on the other end, I could tell
15 they were ticked off by my mood. "Yeah, what do you
16 want?" I nearly snarled into the phone. "What's up with
17 you?" my friend asked. "Well, if you must know, I was about
18 to chomp down on a Three Musketeers bar. I'm holding it in
19 my hot little hand right now." "Well, why can't you eat and
20 talk at the same time?" she asked me. "You don't get it, do
21 you?" I asked her. "There's nothing like the first bite.
22 Nothing can interrupt that. Not a TV show, not a phone call.
23 Nothing. The first bite is almost sacred. It's the moment
24 your taste buds get ahold of perfection. It doesn't get any
25 better than that." There was silence on the other end.
26 Another pause. Maybe I've gone too far. She's really mad at
27 me. She finally talks. She has a confession to make. All
28 that talk about the first bite has gotten to her. "I had to go

1   and get it," she finally said. "Get what?" I asked her. "The
2   chocolate éclair bar I had hidden." "OK, how was the first
3   bite?" I ask. "Heavenly," she said. Now she gets it. Know
4   what I mean? There's nothing like it.

39. The Humor Columnist

1   A laugh a day keeps the doctor away. All right, all right,
2 I know that expression was supposed to say an apple a day
3 keeps the doctor away, but a laugh is even better. My job
4 is to make you laugh. It's not always easy finding the humor
5 in life. In fact, some days are just downright depressing.
6 Naturally a pessimist, my sarcasm reigns, but at least it's
7 in my own court. I just have to slap it around a little and
8 make it behave. There's a thin line between funny and just
9 plain mean. Some comedians fall off the fence toward the
10 mean side, but to each his own. There's a certain redheaded
11 comedienne that comes to mind, but I'm not naming any
12 names. When I sit butt in chair until I write a new humor
13 column each week, I go back over the week's happenings.
14 What is it that I can draw humor from? I used to write about
15 my little brothers and sisters until they got big enough to
16 read what I was writing and then I had to stop. Bummer.
17 They made for some good material, too. Everyday life is ripe
18 with possibilities. For three years I made notes of all the
19 funny things that happened in high school. The result was a
20 book of funny high school stories. I hoped the principal
21 wouldn't kick me out if he got wind of it. Life is stranger
22 than fiction. Give it a try. Study what's going on around you
23 and jot things down. There's bound to be a good blog in
24 there somewhere with some real gems that'll make
25 someone laugh. Tickle your own funny bone. You'll be glad
26 you did.

40. Initials in the Sand

1   *(Holds a sand bucket and a rosary.)*
2   I've walked these beaches many times before, and I've
3   never seen anything like this. See those initials over there?
4   The waves have come and gone over them, but the initials
5   remain. Many people come down here and write their initials
6   in the sand and they wash away in no time. These initials
7   have stood the test of time. I bet they've been there two
8   thousand years. I've seen people come and write their sins
9   in the sand. I guess it's symbolic for confession and the
10 washing away of their sins. It almost makes me want to
11 take Communion when I'm done there. Are you feeling it?
12 Some come back week after week, writing the same sins
13 down in the sand. How many times will they be washed
14 away? How many times can they be forgiven? How many
15 times can someone ask for forgiveness? I guess the waves
16 are a redeeming force. They make all things new. I stop and
17 think about things I've done wrong lately. I stoop and use
18 my finger to etch them in the sand, looking over my
19 shoulder to make sure no one is watching. I don't want to
20 tell all of my secrets now, do I? It takes me awhile to finish
21 writing. Hey, I never said that I was a saint. Looking at what
22 I've written, I secretly hope it will be washed away before
23 someone else comes along. They don't need to know all the
24 dirt on me. A wave comes up and washes away everything
25 I've written. I breath a deep sigh of relief. It works every
26 time. I look back toward the initials that never wash away
27 and I whisper them to myself as I head back to the car.
28 "J.C." I get it now ... *(Walks away, carrying a sand bucket in*
29 *one hand and a rosary in the other.)*

41. The Letter Writer

1 They say that a picture is worth a thousand words.
2 Likewise, a well-written letter can be worth a thousand
3 pictures. I think letter writing is a dying art. How many emails
4 and Facebook messages do you get in a week? Just imagine if
5 all of those expressions were given real time and thought and
6 written out on some nice stationery. You'd really feel rich
7 beyond words, wouldn't you? I have letters that I've saved for
8 ten years. A written note means so much, especially those that
9 come from deep in the heart. I once got a note from Ann
10 Landers. You know, the woman who wrote words of advice in
11 the newspaper? I'd sent her a poem and she wrote back,
12 thanking me for it. It was really moving that she took the time
13 to sit down and write me. But maybe I shouldn't have been so
14 surprised. This was a woman who made her living because
15 people sat down and wrote her letters. I will always cherish that
16 note from her. Another cherished note was a simple postcard
17 from Dave Barry. I'd taken a picture of myself standing in front
18 of the Wright Memorial holding his book that was dedicated to
19 the Wright Brothers. I said the photo was dedicated to the guy
20 who dedicated his book to the guys who dedicated their lives
21 to the skill of flying. Apparently he liked it because he sent me
22 this simple postcard saying, "Thanks! Dave Barry." Now while
23 some would think that he could have written more, I stop to
24 consider that he must get tons of mail from readers; people
25 who really know how to sit down and write a letter. Imagine the
26 possibilities. What celebrity or author would you like to write
27 to? How about a loved one? Get out that pen and get started.
28 Now, while I'm thinking about it ... where's my pen? Have you
29 seen it?

42. The Jilted Bride

1 (A suitcase is in place On-stage.)
2 My name's Denise Fanny. I was looking forward to
3 getting a new last name. But I got jilted. At the altar. I never
4 thought it would happen. Everything was in place. All the
5 attendants and the escorts. The flowers, the food, the folks.
6 Everything. The preacher even showed up on time. I was
7 standing there with my dad, expecting to walk down the
8 aisle, when I saw it. He wasn't standing there by the
9 preacher and the best man. The man I'd thought *was* the
10 best man for me was nowhere in sight. How could he have
11 done this? Through my tears, I looked again, to make sure
12 I wasn't having a hallucination. I think strange things can
13 happen to your mind on your wedding day. So many things
14 can go wrong. But nothing can go more wrong than the
15 groom disappearing. How could he have done it? Left me
16 standing there looking like an idiot? This was all a mistake.
17 Look at all the money I've spent. Hey, I've even heard of a
18 bride suing a defecting groom for standing her up. Now
19 there's a thought. I sue him, get rich, and live happily ever
20 after. I take the money, go on a trip to some tropical island,
21 meet a prince, and get even richer. I feel a big smile come
22 to my face. My dad looks at me like I've lost my mind.
23 Maybe I have. I'm imagining bigger fish in the sea. Then my
24 groom shows up. I feel confused. The tropical island
25 disappears from my mind, and I wonder what went wrong.
26 How could I have thought like that? One minute ready to
27 walk down the aisle, the next ready to blow town with a legal
28 settlement. Money, power, greed. What was wrong with me?

1   He smiles at me. I hold his hand and the ceremony starts.
2   He turns to me and says, "I can't do this." By that time, I
3   am ready for him. I've already mentally booked that flight.
4   *(Grabs suitcase and walks off as the light dims.)*

43. The Kiss

1 (Has lipstick in her pocket. A teddy bear is in place On-stage.)
2 You've seen 'em. You know, those classic kiss pictures.
3 The one where the sailor grabs the nurse and swings her
4 around, planting a big hungry kiss on her. The photographer
5 was in the right place at the right time. Word was, in reality,
6 after the kiss she slapped him. I wish I'd never heard that
7 part. Somehow it took away the romance of that picture. I'd
8 rather have thought that his kiss so melted her that she
9 swooned on the spot. There's another kiss picture that's a
10 classic. Someone who looks like Judge Reinhold is kissing
11 a woman. It's romantic and exciting. Both hang in my office.
12 They're a reminder that true love really does win in the long
13 run. Why the obsession with kiss pictures? It's hard to put
14 into words. I even bought a friend's kiss painting. It hangs
15 in the same room. Always on the lookout for something to
16 stimulate the muse, this works if I'm writing about couples
17 in love. One look at any of these pictures sends the
18 keyboard flying on a romantic trip. If I hung pictures of
19 people fighting, my muse would probably come from either
20 corner, just swinging. They say to surround yourself with
21 things you love and your muse will be happy. Does that ring
22 true for you? Those kiss pictures are definitely something
23 that I love. And so the search is always on for something
24 that gives me a warm fuzzy. And a great kiss — well, that's
25 got warm fuzzy written all over it. (Puts on lipstick and kisses
26 a teddy bear, walking off the stage.)

44. The Mermaid

1   *(Wears a mermaid costume.)*
2   One flip of my tail and you'll be charmed. I'm a
3 mermaid. I guess that just goes without saying. It's pretty
4 obvious that I don't have legs and feet. It's something of a
5 handicap. At the mall, they have a lot of handicap parking
6 spots. What I really need is a trough in which to swim up to
7 the front door. Once I'm inside, I can hop on a scooter and
8 scoot around. If you can't find me, you can just follow the
9 squeal. I know you've seen *Splash*. Who hasn't? I try to
10 avoid the television aisle in the store. I don't want to go
11 busting TV sets. And I don't dare set foot in a pet store. If
12 the aquariums burst from my squealing, there'd be hell to
13 pay. I'm sure of that. You've read all about sirens in *The*
14 *Odyssey*. I'm nothing like that. While my allure is real, I'm
15 not out to hurt you. I'm quite the opposite. My song and my
16 soul are soothing. They aren't out to injure you in any way.
17 I guess you can call me a muse. It goes with the territory.
18 They say that listening to water can be stimulating, too. It
19 kind of stirs up the creative juices. If you're charmed by me,
20 don't be surprised. I've been known to do that. Guys get lost
21 in the fluidity of these baby blues. It's not intentional on my
22 part. It just happens. They hear the siren call and I haven't
23 even made a sound. They dig me, scales and all. Really,
24 there's nothing fishy about that. What's that you say? You
25 don't believe in mermaids? Come on now. For centuries,
26 seamen have claimed such sightings. Next time you're
27 ocean-bound, keep your eyes open. You just never know.
28 *(Lights fade but focus on her tail.)*

45. The Model

1   (Holds a camera.)
2   Hi. My name's Gisele. You may have seen me in a
3   fashion magazine, or maybe not. Depends on what floats
4   your boat. I've always wanted to be a model, ever since I
5   was a little girl. I imagined myself on the pages of *Vogue*
6   magazine, wearing some European fashion, way ahead of
7   style in the States. It takes light years for some of it to
8   reach here, and then there's the trickle-down effect. It took
9   ten years for the jeans with holes in them to hit the streets
10   in the South. No joke. You think I'm kidding, don't you?
11   Modeling for the big designers takes a lot of nerve. Have you
12   seen some of the stuff they come up with? There's no
13   wonder a lot of the models don't smile, excluding, of course,
14   the Victoria's Secret models. They're smiling all over
15   themselves. Well, I guess they are. Being built like that
16   would make anybody smile. Oh well, I ramble. My first
17   modeling job was at the beach for a hotel chain. I wound up
18   modeling in a hot tub with a guy model. Now I ask you, is
19   there any better way to make money? I mean really. They
20   paid me seventy-five dollars an hour, and it was sheer fun.
21   After that, they shot photos of us strolling on the beach
22   together. It wound up printed in brochures, online, and in
23   the yellow pages for two years straight. Of course, that was
24   back in the day. Now my modeling pays me way more than
25   that. I won't tell you how much. You'd be green with envy.
26   And I don't think green would match that outfit you're
27   wearing today. You never know when someone might take
28   *your* picture. Like right now. *(Pulls out a camera.)* **Freeze**
29   **frame!** *(Snaps a photo and walks off the stage.)*

46. The Mug

1   I don't know how many coffees I've had. Isn't that
2   pathetic? My heart's pounding like a drum. I'd say that I've
3   had five cups. Problem is, I'm waiting for this guy to show
4   up. I met him online. Go ahead and say it. "Breena, it's not
5   safe to do that. A girl could get killed" or something. I've
6   seen couples come and go in here. They come in and order
7   pizza and wait for it to be cooked. I sit and look at my
8   watch, wondering if he'll show. An hour has gone by, and
9   I've given him the benefit of the doubt. Maybe he had a flat
10   tire. Maybe his mom went to the hospital. Maybe he really
11   has a girlfriend and didn't have the heart to tell me. For all
12   I know, he could have been one of the guys who just left
13   here with a girl. I'm not sure. All I know is that I'm bonding
14   with my coffee mug, drowning my insecurities in a cup of
15   joe. The cook is kind of cute. Maybe if he doesn't show up,
16   I'll return something I order to the cook so he'll make a
17   special trip out here to see me. Just me and nobody else. I
18   brought my own mug. It kind of draws attention to me, and
19   it's also my good luck charm. It has a picture of a Kincaid
20   painting on it. You know, the guy who captures light with his
21   painting. There's a painting of a quaint cottage on it with
22   the light gleaming. Just as I lose myself in the image, I feel
23   a hand on my shoulder. I look up and see the kindest blue
24   eyes I've ever seen. My eyes travel upward to see blonde
25   hair and a boyish grin. "I'm sorry I'm late," he says. I set
26   my mug down and smile. My heart dances. Is it the five cups
27   of coffee I downed while waiting for him to show up, or is it
28   love at first sight? *(Sighs and runs off the stage.)*

47. The Little Black Dress

1   *(Wears a black dress.)*

2   I knew it was the right dress as soon as I saw it. Nothing
3 knocks them out like the LBD, otherwise known as the little
4 black dress. You've seen 'em. Those classy frocks that show
5 up at parties and weddings. The ones that you can either
6 dress up or dress down, depending on your mood. It looked
7 so good on me at the store. Of course my best friend
8 Chelsea didn't tell me she liked it. She secretly coveted that
9 dress. I know she did. I could tell by the way she smiled with
10 one side of her mouth. I found the perfect shoes to go with
11 it. Do you know how hard that is? To find shoes that go so
12 well with it you think you'd died and gone to heaven? So,
13 the night of the party, I show up in this dress. Every head
14 in the place turned and looked at me. I never felt so special
15 in my life. There was this whisper and a hushed silence
16 came over the entire party. Wow, I thought. I was beaming
17 from ear to ear. I felt like a real princess in that LBD. I really
18 outdid myself this time, I thought. Everything was going well
19 until Chelsea pulled me aside and into the bathroom. I
20 looked into the mirror. The dress looked fine. In fact, it
21 looked more than fine. It looked spectacular. Was something
22 wrong? Why was everybody looking at me? And then I saw
23 it. Ever so softly, a bird had flown over and taken a dump in
24 my hair. You know, I thought I felt something warm up there
25 but didn't give it another thought. The LBD couldn't
26 compete with that for attention. You know, now every time I
27 look at that LBD I'll remember that night. Those initials
28 have come to stand for something new. Look, bird
29 droppings! *(Screams, throws hands up, and runs out.)*

48. The Look

1　Two simple words: the look. I know the look when I see
2　it. I'm a talent agent. I send my little darlin's on model
3　shoots and acting gigs. When I see someone who has the
4　look, I know it immediately. Just the other day I saw this
5　guy with the greatest profile. There was no doubt about it.
6　He had it. Without question. I told him to send me his
7　headshot. There's a certain grace about some potential
8　models. Something that screams, "Shoot me." Not with a
9　gun, but with a camera. They possess an innate sense
10　about how to pose, how to make the camera love them. It's
11　a gift. I don't even have to tell them how to stand or sit. I
12　love working with them. Sometimes I find the perfect model
13　walking through a mall. They aren't even aware that they
14　have it. They're usually surprised and somewhat humble
15　when I hand them my business card, asking them to call
16　me. That's the most beautiful part. They really didn't have
17　a clue. Other times I find them doing something they enjoy
18　doing, like running or surfing. I never know where I might
19　find the world's next superstar. It could be at the grocery
20　store or sitting in a sports bar. With a camera hanging
21　around my neck, I ask if I can photograph people. I get weird
22　looks, but in the long run, it's worth it. I'm always in search
23　of the look. Oh, by the way, are you busy? Mind if I take
24　your picture? There's something about you. I think you've
25　got it. You've got the look.

49. The Massage Therapist

1   You've probably met me before. I'm a massage
2   therapist. Well, if you're lucky you've met me. I have hands
3   to die for. I'm the woman who knows how to rub your
4   shoulders in just the right way to make you melt. If you're
5   having a hard day, I can make it all better. Muscles knot up
6   around your shoulders and they can be pounded and
7   kneaded away, and in no time flat, you're feeling like a new
8   person. When did I realize that I wanted to be a massage
9   therapist? Somewhere along the way, I realized that I liked
10 the sense of touch. My friends would be having a bad day
11 and I'd help them relax by rubbing their shoulders. They
12 were putty in my hands. I wound up with more good lunch
13 desserts than you can imagine with my skill. Of course, I
14 couldn't do this at school. Any touchy-feely stuff is off limits
15 there. So I'd give them a massage on the way home on the
16 bus. What, you're worried about the bus driver? She got a
17 massage, too. Heaven knows she needed it at the end of the
18 ride, and my house was the last one on the list. It came in
19 handy. I wound up with more school supplies and good food
20 just because my fingers worked magic. I never did anything
21 but the shoulders on any friends, but they were always
22 grateful. That's when I knew that I had a gift, a gift that
23 keeps on giving. When I got older, I took a class in massage
24 therapy. Turns out there was so much to learn about it, but
25 the most important thing I learned is that when you do it,
26 people are eternally grateful that you helped them relax. It's
27 so worth it. If all I got paid was a smile and seeing a spring
28 in their step, then I've made a difference. So what do you
29 say? Feeling tense?

50. The Teacher

1   So many papers to grade. Whew! And how much sleep
2 did I get last night? My head hurts, but I'm standing outside
3 the classroom door greeting everyone as they enter. I like to
4 speak to every student as they come in. That way they'll
5 know they really matter to me. Did you know that? That you
6 really matter to me? I'm not just saying that. I think about
7 you when you walk out of my room and into the rest of your
8 life here or at home. Maybe you get labeled for the things
9 you do. Maybe you have ADHD and have no clue that the
10 word "consequences" even exists. Well, I'm an undiagnosed
11 ADD kind of person myself. I know when my body says, hey,
12 it's been at least forty-five minutes here, let's bolt. I
13 understand more than you know. I see the look in your eye
14 when your boyfriend or girlfriend dumps you. Maybe I won't
15 call on you to give me answers when I see that look. It's
16 kind of a deer-caught-in-the-headlights stare. Believe it or
17 not, I've had that stare before myself. When everyone else
18 thinks you're a bad seed, I will seek out that spark in you
19 that makes you shine when no one else has. The worst of
20 the worst even have something worthwhile to share. Just
21 last week I saw a student who, years ago, everyone had
22 given up on, and I helped him finish a paper to graduate. He
23 came up to me with a huge grin on his face. Then he told
24 me about how he was in college now. He thanked me for
25 helping him in school. Just thinking about that has made
26 my head feel better already. *(Turns head and says)* Well, good
27 morning ... come on in and have a seat.

About the Author

Phyllis Johnson is an author, photojournalist, professional artist, and sometimes actress living in eastern Virginia. Her roles have included parts in *New Detectives, FBI Files, Diagnosis Unknown, Psychic Investigator,* Discovery Channel's movie of the week and an independent film, *Sweet Good Fortune.* Admittedly, her strangest acting experience was a role on 6/6/06 (666) in *Psychic Investigator* — the "Possessed Investigator" episode about a possessed woman. The set was a makeshift church, and a thunderstorm raged outside. It was a truly surreal night for her.

Phyllis has also written for and performed at the Smithfield Little Theatre in Smithfield, Virginia in their annual One Acts Festival. Check out her website at www.phyllisjohnson.net to read about her books: *inkBLOT,* a young adult suspense novel co-written under the pen name Johnson Naigle with Nancy Naigle; *Being Frank with Anne,* a poetic interpretation of Anne Frank's diary (she even got it reviewed by Anne's cousin, Buddy Elias, and is thrilled to have a copy signed by Miep Gies); *Twelve is for More than Doughnuts,* poetry and essays based on the Bible; *Poetic Dreamer,* poems inspired by art, photography, and life in general; and her first book, *Hot and Bothered by It,* a book of midlife humorous poetry.

Order Form

Meriwether Publishing Ltd.
PO Box 7710
Colorado Springs, CO 80933-7710
Phone: 800-937-5297 Fax: 719-594-9916
Website: www.meriwether.com

Please send me the following books:

_____	**Just Me #BK-B353**	**$16.95**
	by Phyllis C. Johnson	
	100 monologues for teens	
_____	**50/50 Monologues for Student Actors #BK-B321**	**$15.95**
	by Mary Depner	
	100 monologues for guys and girls	
_____	**50/50 Monologues for Student Actors II #BK-B330**	**$16.95**
	by Mary Depner	
	100 more monologues for guys and girls	
_____	**102 Great Monologues #BK-B315**	**$16.95**
	by Rebecca Young	
	A versatile collection of monologues and duologues for student actors	
_____	**Famous Fantasy Character Monologs #BK-B286**	**$16.95**
	by Rebecca Young	
	Starring the Not-So-Wicked Witch and more	
_____	**102 Monologues for Middle School Actors #BK-B327**	**$17.95**
	by Rebecca Young	
	Including comedy and dramatic monologues	
_____	**Improv Ideas #BK-B283**	**$24.95**
	by Justine Jones and Mary Ann Kelley	
	A book of games and lists	

These and other fine Meriwether Publishing books are available at your local bookstore or direct from the publisher. Prices subject to change without notice. Check our website or call for current prices.

Name: _____ email:_____

Organization name: _____

Address: _____

City: _____ State: _____

Zip: _____ Phone: _____

❑ **Check enclosed**

❑ **Visa / MasterCard / Discover / Am. Express #** _____

Signature: _____ *Expiration date:* _____ / _____ *CVV code:* _____
(required for credit card orders)

Colorado residents: Please add 3% sales tax.
Shipping: Include $3.95 for the first book and 75¢ for each additional book ordered.

❑ *Please send me a copy of your complete catalog of books and plays.*